Keith Howard & John A. Sharp

THE MANAGEMENT OF A STUDENT RESEARCH PROJECT

Gower

Published by
Gower Publishing
Gower House
Croft Road
Aldershot
Hampshire GU11 3HR

Reprinted 1985, 1986, 1987, 1989, 1991, 1992, 1993

British Library Cataloguing in Publication Data

Howard, Keith
    The management of a student research project.
    1. Universities and colleges—Graduate work
    I. Title   II. Sharp, John A.
    378'.170281   LB2371

ISBN 0 566 00613 8

Printed and bound in Great Britain at
the University Press, Cambridge

Contents

vi

2

Selecting and Justifying a Research Topic 21

3

Planning the Research Project 46

4

Literature Searching 67

PART B: DATA ANALYSIS AND GATHERING

5

Analysing the Data   99

6

Gathering the Data   121

PART C: PRODUCING THE RESEARCH RESULTS

7

Executing the Research   151

8

Presentation of the Research Findings   174

Epilogue   213

Appendices

General bibliography   227

Index   233

List of Figures and Tables

Figures

Tables

Preface

The expansion of tertiary education during the last twenty years has seen a significant growth in the number of courses during which the student is expected to undertake project work of one form or another. Although not always designated as 'research' a large proportion, if indeed not the majority, of projects require independent enquiry on the part of the student which would qualify for that description. It is hoped that this book will have something for all students whose aim is to write up and present for examination the results of projects which may last from a month or two to several years.

The aim of the book is to assist such students to manage their projects both more efficiently and more effectively. The motivation to write the book came over three years spent by the authors as Chairman and Vice-Chairman of the large doctoral programme at the University of Bradford Management Centre and their experiences as supervisors and examiners of full and part-time students working on doctoral and master's theses, master's dissertations, and undergraduate projects.

Responsibility for the co-ordination of the activities of well over 100 research degree students during these three years made it clear that although the students may be working on widely differing topics they shared many problems in common. By reflecting on the experiences of students in various fields and at various levels the authors concluded that a book which was concerned with the *management* of a student research project rather than with the problems arising from a particular field of research itself should have general relevance. Although the discussion must cater for the highest (that is doctoral) level it was felt that much guidance could be obtained by selective reading of the book by the student working at first degree level.

For projects which are given a mark or must be completed if a qualification is to be awarded the objective of the student is quite clear. At research degree level however, the situation, until quite recently, has been very different, with the so-called 'apprentice model' influencing attitudes. At its best the apprentice model involves a student working under the direction of a single academic who in addition to being an expert in the area of the study is skilled in research methodology and is able to motivate the student to complete his thesis within a prescribed time. At its worst it implies incompetent and inadequate supervision with both student and supervisor being responsible to no-one in particular and resulting in yet another 'failure to complete'.

Although there is a slow trend to central direction or co-ordination of student research it remains the case that the vast majority of students will depend largely for success on their own resources and, as stated, it is the aim of the authors to improve both the standard of the research and the probability of timely completion of the written report by promoting self-management. Our current working environment means that we draw heavily on the social sciences for examples but hope that our earlier backgrounds in engineering and mathematics (together with not a few years in industry) will enable us to establish credibility to student researchers in a much wider field.

We have tried out our ideas on a number of colleagues and would like to express our sincere thanks to Dr Stephen Sobol and Virginia Hayden in particular who caused us to do quite a bit of rethinking. Our gratitude is extended also to Pat Corby and Nigel Howard who were kind enough to criticise certain passages, and to Anne Bennett who offered us some advice on reproduction. Additionally we recognise the valuable assistance received from the Management Centre Librarian, Neil Hunter.

A quite separate and distinct expression of thanks should be made to Marjorie Richards who compiled the first draft of the manuscript for us.

Coping with contributions from two authors is by no means easy, and quite apart from typing the text she did on occasions undertake duties of a sub-editorial nature.

Our thanks are similarly extended to Majorie Kay for undertaking the heavy work involved in incorporating the final amendments into the text.

As a final point we hope that our female readers will not be offended by our use of the masculine form.

K. Howard

J. A. Sharp

PART A:
PREPARATION

Research and the Research Student

THE AIM OF THIS BOOK

Many degree and diploma students become involved in projects of one form or another. In some instances the project forms part of a course, in other cases the project is virtually the whole basis on which the degree is awarded.

Whether the student is seeking to write a report at undergraduate level, a dissertation at master's level, or a thesis at doctoral level, two key factors which must be borne in mind are timing and quality. In some instances the time constraint is inflexible; if the report is not presented by a particular date the qualification desired is not obtained. When deadlines of this nature apply, compliance with them can lead to content which is sub-standard.

PhD and master's theses must be of high quality and recognition of this often results in inordinate lengths of time being taken for completion. Indeed the task of finishing theses proves to be too much for many students and was the subject of some discussion in the UK national press during early 1981 (see for example *The Times*, 15 January 1981). It was found that although achievement was a little better in the subject areas covered by the then Science Research Council (now the Science and Engineering Research Council – SERC) only about 30 per cent of students who had been researching full-time in the Social Sciences were awarded higher degrees (in some cases up to a decade after commencing their studies).

It is assumed that admission procedures ensure that, in the main, student entrants have the potential to complete their studies satisfactorily. What, therefore, are the reasons why sub-standard work is submitted or students fail to complete? Much of the explanation must lie in the inability of the student to plan and control, that is *manage* his work. And by *manage* we mean the manipulation of all resources available to him, both material and human. The most important of the latter being the person who in many cases is designated to supervise the student.

Our aim is to provide degree and diploma students (and their supervisors) with guidance in the identification of research projects and on how to complete them.

It is recognised that the demands made of students in terms of training and quality will vary enormously according to the level at which the research is undertaken, but it is argued that all research projects have certain features in common. We feel, though, that it would be unsatisfactory to adopt an 'average' approach and thus will attempt to satisfy the needs of the highest level of student research. It is hoped that students working at other levels will be able to find the guidance apposite for them, skimming over those sections of the chapters that are particularly pertinent for research degree students. Where possible the book is addressed to all types of student researcher and will often refer to the 'research report' rather than to 'thesis, dissertation, or report', but if the remarks are directed specifically to the research degree student 'thesis' will be employed.

Some of the particular needs of the part-time student are considered where these differ from those of the full-time student.

THE STRUCTURE OF THE BOOK

Almost by definition research is not a straightforward process made up of a series of distinct steps each of which is part of a clearly defined sequence. Quite apart from opportunities to undertake several activities at the same time blind alleys will from time to time necessitate a return to an earlier stage. This does not mean, however, that the student should use the inevitability of uncertainty as an excuse for not adopting a systematic and logical approach to his work. The latter is the essence of planning; itself a vital part of management.

This book has been divided into three parts each of which is concerned with a broad aspect of student research. It can be argued that certain activities are more or less common to research regardless of the field in which it is pursued. Thus all students have to select (or at the very least understand the implications of) a topic. They will then need to use the particular skills and techniques which the specific nature of their research demands. Finally, they will have to undertake their work within a certain environment before reporting upon the outcome of their studies. Figure 1.1 shows the extent to which it is possible to cover in a book aimed at research students in general the range of problems encountered by the student at each of these stages of his research.

The inference to be drawn from Figure 1.1 is that both the preparation and production phases of student research have (for a given level) much that is common across all research fields. That which primarily distinguishes one type of research from another are the activities needed to track down, collect, and analyse data. The latter, as depicted in Figure 1, are the subject of Part B which comprises the chapters on analysing the data, and gathering the data. In addition to the present chapter the other chapters to be found in Part A are selecting and justifying a research topic, planning the research project and literature searching. Part C which is concerned with research output includes chapters on executing the research and presenting the results of the research.

Part B presented the greatest difficulty in our attempt to be relevant to the broad field of student research. We have however concentrated on the management of data gathering and analysis. In our coverage of analytical methods we recognise our bias towards the social sciences but would claim that many of the techniques referred to have a broader application.

We shall also consider some of the particular needs of the part-time student where these differ from those of the full-time student.

We do not propose that this book should be read from cover to cover at one go; much will depend on the experience which has been accumulated by the student. Sections of the book have been designed to impart skills (such as those needed in literature searching and formal planning), others to add to the student's knowledge (for example the chapter on analytical techniques), and still others to describe the environment in which the research will be conducted (for example the problems encountered in executing research). Thus the book may be seen as a reference work, to be picked up at intervals during the course of the study.

WHAT IS RESEARCH?

Most people associate the word 'research' with activities which are substantially removed from day-to-day life and which are pursued by outstandingly gifted persons with an unusual level of commitment. There is of course a good deal of truth in this viewpoint, but we would argue that the pursuit is not restricted to this type of person and indeed can prove to be a stimulating and satisfying experience for many people with a trained and enquiring mind.

It is the case that the major contributions to knowledge do tend to come from highly intelligent and committed investigators. Significant advances are, however, the 'tip of the iceberg' insofar as the total volume of effort is concerned. Indeed, top class investigators often fail to achieve firm conclusions, while by far the greatest amount of activity is much less ambitious in nature. Fundamental additions to knowledge frequently draw upon prior studies of restricted scope carried out perhaps by workers of only limited research experience.

Thus if it is accepted that lower level work and training are prerequisites for the expansion of knowledge it would seem that 'research' is an activity which can be undertaken at any time in an individual's life when reasoned thinking is possible.

We define research as:

seeking through methodical processes to add to one's own body of knowledge and, hopefully, to that of others, by the discovery of non-trivial facts and insights

At the higher levels of student research a necessary condition of success is that the research actually adds to existing knowledge rather than simply leading to an increase in an individual's understanding of previous work. This requirement will be considered at some length in the next chapter.

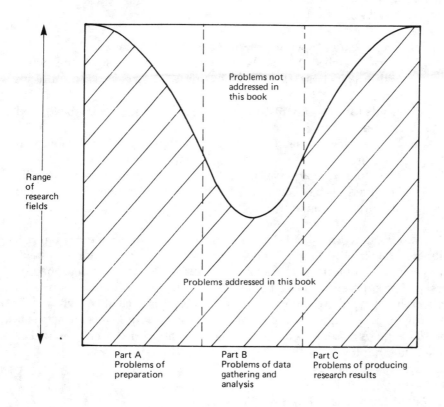

Figure 1.1   The extent to which problems common to a range of student research are addressed in this book

SOME FEATURES OF STUDENT RESEARCH

The concern of this book is with student research projects and although a commonness of process is evident account must be taken of constraints which are imposed by the particular environment in which the student will be working. For example all or some of the following factors may be relevant.

1. The research topic may be imposed on the student.
2. The research (if it is to be rated a success) must be completed within a given time period: for example four weeks, six months, or three years.
3. Funds for experiments, travel, postage and so on may be limited or non existent.
4. The results of the research must be presented in a specified manner.
5. The student may have to relate to an academic supervisor who may possibly be disinterested or lacking in competence in the field of study chosen.

Research work outside the educational system is almost entirely directed towards adding to knowledge. Within the educational system, however, an additonal factor is present, namely the need to demonstrate research competence. Indeed at all levels, except the higher degrees by research, the need to demonstrate research competence outweighs that of adding to knowledge. Short comments on the various levels are apposite at this stage. A closer look at the criteria to be satisfied at each level will be taken in Chapter 8.

First Degree and Diploma Projects

This category includes studies which form part of courses at the first level of further education, many of which are referred to as 'degree equivalent'. Although analytical rigour is not usually demanded independent enquiry and exercise of judgement is expected as is a reasonable standard of presentation of the results. It is customary for the projects to comprise part of the student's assessment. Rarely will projects represent less than ten per cent of a particular year's assessment. In some instances (for example the sandwich course with a whole year in industry) the project may be the only academic assessment made.

It may be argued that if students are capable of independent enquiry they should also be capable of planning how the enquiry should be pursued. There is some force to this but what is often not appreciated by tutor or student is that there is much more to research methodology than may initially be supposed. Time devoted to studying the research process is therefore a worthwhile investment.

Although research is a vital element of further education it should not be assumed that all tutors have themselves had research experience. True, academic staff may have been overseeing first degree or diploma projects for many years but this does not guarantee competence in research methods.

Postgraduate Dissertations

A fairly recent feature has been the growth in master's degrees obtained by 'study and dissertation'. Thus typically a one year's full-time course may comprise nine months of taught courses, with three months being available for a project to be written up as a dissertation. A period of the order of three months is insufficient to enable tasks to be undertaken which will form a sufficient basis for the 'thesis' required for the master's or doctoral research degrees. Little more than a descriptive account can be given of some line of enquiry; the absence of validation and generalisation distinguishing the dissertation from the thesis of the pure research degrees.

In those instances where the elapsed time made available for a postgraduate dissertation is rigidly controlled the student needs to plan his project very carefully and in particular should avoid being over ambitious. There are however some courses which permit a student to take much longer over his dissertation (possibly an additional two or more years). Although in some instances the dissertation will then be more substantial due to a greater opportunity to collect data the probability of completion can be reduced by the competing demands of employment.

Masters' Degree by Research

The requirements for the successful completion of projects at this level are in some respects difficult to establish. In particular the degree of originality needed and the extent to which generalisation of the results is possible may be unclear. At the very least any conclusions which are reached must be capable of validation even if no attempt to generalise them is made. Certainly the contribution to knowledge of a master's thesis should be of some significance, particularly in view of the fact that it is likely to serve as a reference work.

The thesis will probably be externally assessed when attention will be given to the thoroughness of the research as indicated by the bibliography, in addition to the analysis, conclusions, and the standard of layout.

Doctoral Projects

This is the highest level of student research activity and although students may go on into careers in research itself this will probably be the last occasion when they are formally assessed on the grounds of both research competence and originality. The major aim is to present a thesis for external assessment which will prove to be satisfactory in both respects. A subsequent aim may be, through publication, to become recognised as an expert in the field of study chosen.

The requirements are, inevitably, more demanding than those of the master's degree by research; for example the University of Bradford (1981) requires that 'The thesis . . . must form a distinct contribution to the knowledge of the subject and show evidence of the discovery of new facts or the exercise of independent judgement'

The achievement of a doctorate in any subject will represent a major investment in terms of time and effort. Rarely is the process completed in less than three years and there is no guarantee of a successful outcome. Failure to complete is a disturbing feature of doctoral study and a major aim of this book as stated earlier is to reduce the frequency of this occurring.

A sizeable proportion of students registered for' doctorates (and indeed for other qualifications) pursue their studies part-time; that is in addition to their prime employment. The motivation needed to sustain research effort over, possibly, a seven year period has to be of a high order. Access to facilities and supervisors are much more restricted than is the case with full-time students and the value of self-management of the project is therefore greater.

CLASSIFYING RESEARCH

The majority of student research projects are completed without much thought being given to the type of study which has been followed.

The research is examined from four points of view each of which will have a different bearing on the successful management and completion of a study.

The Field of Research

Research is most frequently classified by field but this is largely little more than a labelling device which enables groups of researchers with similar interests to be identified.

Fields are often grouped for administrative purposes into categories such as the social sciences, life sciences, physical sciences, engineering, and the humanities, and a small proportion of research may fall into more than one of these categories. This is particularly so at the higher levels of research where the project may often involve the translation of ideas from one field to another.

As far as this book is concerned classification by field is of the least relevance. This does not mean that the researcher does not need a comprehensive knowledge of his own subject. Rather it reflects our intention to concentrate on aspects of research that are common to most fields and the majority of research projects.

The Purpose of Research

There are many different purposes of a research project. Four common ones are:

a) to review existing knowledge;
b) to describe some situation or problem;
c) the construction of something novel;
d) explanation.

The review of existing research findings is a very common type of student research project. It can provide excellent research training with the added advantage that it requires little by way of resources save access to a good library.

Although descriptive research may appear to be less demanding than other types this is often far from the case. However, due to the lack of knowledge of subject or research methods, or both, it is quite possible that the purpose of a student's first study will be to describe something.

The construction of something which is useful is an ultimate outcome of research which increasingly is being favoured by sponsors. In the physical sciences and engineering, students may be recruited to pursue a particular line of research such as the construction of a new type of optical system.

Explanation is the ideal of all professional research workers. It is only when causal rather than statistical relationships are identified that generalisations may be made or laws formulated.

The Approach to Research

Another way of classifying research is by the major research approach used. Some approaches that are frequently used in student research are the laboratory experiment; the field experiment; the case study; and the survey.

The *laboratory experiment* is relevant to all the major research groupings (with the possible exception of the humanities) but is primarily used in physical science, life science, and engineering research.

In the context of research method a *field experiment* suggests that an investigation subjected to certain controls is conducted in non-laboratory conditions. For example, a new detergent may have been developed as a result of laboratory research and a field experiment may be set up to see how well it works in actual use.

The *case study* is often the basis for student projects, particularly in the social sciences. In this type of research a student may spend a period in an organisation and the comments and conclusions which emerge will be based solely on his experiences in that setting.

There is some connection between the field experiment and the *survey* in that techniques relevant to the latter may be used in the former. However. whereas the field experiment implies controls and need not necessarily involve people the survey is viewed separately here as a method of extracting attitudes and opinions from a sizeable sample of respondents.

The Nature of Research

Our last view of research is variation by nature and type of contribution to knowledge. Grinyer (1981)[1] has suggested four types

---

1. Professor P. H. Grinyer who is head of the Economics Department at the University of St Andrews put these views forward at the 5th National Conference on Doctoral Research in Management and Industrial Relations. The conference was held at the University of Aston Management Centre on 6/7 April 1981.

Pure theory;
Testing of existing theory;
Description of the state of the art;
Specific problem solution.

The particular interest of this typology is that Grinyer's view of a PhD in the field of management is that the opportunity of a truly original contribution to knowledge (which is related to our concept of value presented in Chapter 2) *decreases,* whereas the chance of successful completion *increases,* as we go down the list. Whilst it will be appreciated that Grinyer's discussion relates principally to doctoral studies in management, nevertheless it raises questions that are important in other fields and at other levels of research.

THE PROCESS OF RESEARCH

Deeper understanding of research will come from consideration of the *process* by which it is conducted and of course from embarking upon an actual study.

We would argue that despite the wide variety of field, purpose, and approach some common features of the research process can be identified; and that if a student departs significantly from a general systematic approach the research will be inefficient and quite possibly ineffectual.

Several conceptual models designed to serve as a basis for a systematic approach to research have been proposed. Rummel and Ballaine (1963) drawing upon suggestions made by J. L. Kelly in 1932 and J. Dewey in 1933 proposed a model with six steps: a felt need, the problem, the hypothesis, collection of data, concluding belief, and general value of conclusion. The model outlined in Figure 1.2 demonstrates some similarities with Rummel and Ballaine's proposal but contains different emphases. Steps 1 to 4 of the model may be described as the *planning phase,* with the remaining steps, numbers 5 to 7 as the *effectuation phase.* Much work, notably a search of the literature, is involved in the first phase, and this should be highly relevant to parts of the second phase. Until the end of step 4 however, it is often the case that the researcher finds it necessary to return to one of the earlier steps before proceeding further. Reversion from the effectuation to the planning phase may, however, prejudice the prospects of completion given the time constraints within which students must work.

14

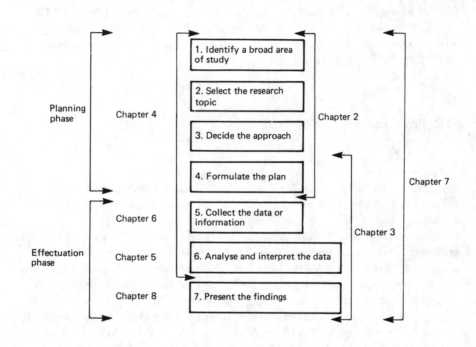

Figure 1.2   A systematic approach to research – a process model

Each step should in fact be viewed as being less reversible as progress is made from the beginning of the project to the end. A research project, however, always involves novelty – at least for the student – and the researcher will frequently find a need to return to an earlier step because later experience has shown how the project can be more closely defined. It will be appreciated that such a return, though it may expedite future work, does not constitute progress. Too frequent reversion to earlier steps is a sure sign that the initial steps of the planning phase have been inadequately carried out.

The seven steps in Figure 1.2 should be comprehensible to all students though the relative importance of individual stages will differ from one project to another according to the aims and approach as we shall see later. The figure contains reference to Chapters 2 to 8 indicating where each of the steps will be considered in some depth. Although during a project the research plan will precede data collection and analysis, these two latter steps are treated earlier in this book so that the student will have an understanding of the methodology and tools of research before he decides upon the direction and duration of his study.

Careful compliance with the model should considerably improve the prospects of successfully completing a piece of research. It is difficult to avoid the temptation to skip steps or to proceed having only partially completed stages. Thus the research topic may have been only vaguely formulated but a student may commence to organise a project in the hope that an appropriate topic will emerge after data have been collected. Or a researcher may reach conclusions after collecting only part of the data planned and, as a result, discontinue further collection, only to find that his inital interpretation was incorrect.

THE SUCCESSFUL COMPLETION OF STUDENT RESEARCH

One immediate question is: What is success? Below master's level this is measured by formal recognition that examination requirements have been satisfied. At master's and doctoral level, when dissertations and theses are to be displayed in libraries, success often means also that the student is satisfied that his own standards have been met.

A further question is what are the factors that affect success as thus defined? A useful vehicle for providing an answer is a survey of PhD students in which the authors were involved in 1981. Stimulated by the widespread concern over completion rates (particularly in the Social

Sciences) the Doctoral Committee at the University of Bradford Management Centre devised a questionnaire and sent this to 45 students whose full-time studies had terminated prior to the 1978/79 session, and to 28 full-time students who were currently doing research. Nineteen replies (42 per cent) were received from the former category and 18 (64 per cent) from the latter. The 19 students who had ceased to research full-time included 10 who had transferred to part-time registration in an endeavour to complete their studies.

Students were asked to indicate for 20 factors whether these had affected research progress beneficially, neutrally, or adversely. The factors included 'the subject chosen', 'the research design', 'quality of supervision', 'quantity of supervison', 'availability of funds', 'teaching', 'running tutorials', 'writing papers', 'attending conferences', 'own level of motivation', and 'own abilities'. The implications of these and other factors will be examined in other parts of this book, particularly in Chapter 7.

In order to effect a measure of interpretation beneficial responses were scored +1, neutral responses O, and adverse responses −1. By simple addition a total score was obtained for each factor, and factors were on this basis assigned to the categories of those having an adverse effect on progress and those having a beneficial effect. The results are shown in Figure 1.3 ranked for each category in descending order.

In Chapter 7 obstacles to successful completion are examined under four different types of problem: individual centred, supervisor related, research related, and general support (see Figure 7.1). Different perceptions will be noted from the above rankings, where for example successful students rated four individually centred activities as having been most beneficial to completion. It should be borne in mind that the rankings were derived from a total of 37 responses and that the point of the exercise was to provide, rapidly, a basis for action. Nevertheless the information derived was interesting and reference will be made again to the survey later in the book. Of some interest here is that only in the case of students who were currently researching full-time was the subject chosen fairly beneficial to progress. Even for those who had successfully completed their studies the factor was located no higher than the mid point of the rankings. As might be expected the nature of the subject chosen was ranked even lower (twelfth of twenty) following the aggregation of the responses of erstwhile full-time students who had yet to complete their research.

	Category of respondent		
	Students who had completed their doctorates	Ex full-time students who had not yet completed	Current full-time students
Factors judged adverse	None	Availability of funds Research design	Teaching Running tutorials
Leading factors judged beneficial	Own level of motivation Own abilities Writing papers Attending conferences Quality of supervision	Writing papers Own abilities Quality of supervision Quantity of supervision Own level of motivation	Attending conferences Own level of motivation Quality of supervision Writing papers The subject chosen

Figure 1.3   A survey response indicating factors which influence student research progress

TYPES OF RESEARCH AND THIS BOOK

Having examined research from four different viewpoints it will be noted that only in one case was it necessary to refer to the subject of the research. Even when research is classified by field, in fact, there are still many acceptable styles of research project.

This in our view justifies our attempt to produce a book that meets the large number of needs that are common to most student researchers. In particular we have drawn heavily on the process model of research (Figure 1.2) in the organisation of the remaining chapters.

This chapter commenced with a reference to the two key factors of timing and quality, and the implications of being unable to satisfy the former are readily apparent – no report, no qualification. We believe that by the adoption of careful management the prospects of earlier and successful completion will be much enhanced.

What is more difficult to grasp is how the quality criterion can be satisfied and, indeed, how it can be measured. It should be evident from studying the different types of research that many varieties exist. There are for example, many combinations of research approach and purpose that are legitimate in a particular field and each will carry with it different implications in terms of constraints and opportunities for research with potential quality. Which is selected will depend in part on student prefer-ence and attitude towards risk. An important point to stress is that as far as is possible the topic should be chosen by the student rather than being foisted upon him, otherwise motivation (which was rated highly in the survey referred to above) will be difficult to sustain.

In Chapter 8 we shall be considering the range of requirements which need to be satisfied at the different levels of research. These will provide a fairly specific list of criteria against which a prospective topic can be evaluated. A rather different view of quality will be taken in Chapter 2 when we will suggest that research may be judged in terms of its potential value and the surprise element which will arise from a change in previ-ously held beliefs. Clearly research which is likely to be rated lowly in terms of both value and surprise will have limited prospects of success at research degree level, even though the methodological quality proved to be high.

An important factor that needs to be taken into account in assessing quality is that value and surprise do not exist in isolation – they are subjective. The need for the student to give some thought to the person or the type of person who will assess the research is pointed to.

The aim should, therefore, be to maximise the probability of timely and successful completion by identifying as soon as possible a research topic with high potential quality. This, taking account of the resources available to the student, should appear, with good management, to be capable of being concluded within whatever period is available to him. As in good management the identification and control of quality is just as important as the planning and control of resources. All of these aspects are examined in the chapters which follow.

SUMMARY

RESEARCH IS: a process by which the researcher extends his knowledge and possibly that of the whole community. Student research is encountered from first degree or diploma level through to doctoral level.
It involves the development of research competence and additions to knowledge. In general the former is more important at lower levels, the latter at higher levels.

RESEARCH CAN BE CLASSIFIED: by field
by purpose
by approach
by nature
Combinations of these categories create a large number of different types of research project. Not all are feasible for any particular student given his expertise and the resources and time available to him.

THE IDENTIFICATION OF A GOOD RESEARCH TOPIC: requires that thought be devoted to its quality which will be assessed by taking into account such factors as standards, value and the element of surprise.

A SUCCESSFUL OUTCOME TO THE RESEARCH PROJECT: is more likely if it is conducted as a series of logically ordered steps which in large part are common to all types of student study. A range of factors (many of which are under the personal control of the student) will have a bearing on the outcome.

2

Selecting and Justifying a Research Topic

TOPIC SELECTION IN OUTLINE

Until a topic has been selected the research cannot be said to be underway. Despite this obvious comment it is not uncommon to find full-time research students who have yet to make a real start on their study a year after commencement. True, they may have done an enormous amount of reading, thinking, or travelling, but in no sense could this be seen as making significant progress which only really occurs from Step 3 of Figure 1.2 onwards. Research plans may founder because of the unexpected but this possibility should not be confused with an inability to identify an appropriate topic with reasonable speed, yet, in our experience, this is one of the most common problems encountered in student research.

The prospects of selecting a suitable topic will be enhanced if a systematic approach is adopted. Figure 2.1 expands primarily upon step 2 of Figure 1.2. In the first place the broad area of study will suggest likely supervisors, who normally will prefer to supervise studies in fields which are related to their main interests. Thus a lecturer in marketing who has inclinations towards quantitative methods may be prepared to undertake supervision of a student who wishes to develop a mathematical advertising model but he may not be prepared to supervise a student who wishes to research into the development of consumerism.

The significance of the various stages included in Figure 2.1 will vary considerably according to the level at which the research is to be undertaken. At one extreme an undergraduate may be presented with a research topic (such as an analysis of a company's distribution system) which would obviate the need for thought to be given to any of the stages. By contrast each of these stages will feature prominently during the early part of a doctoral study, consuming perhaps 20 per cent of the time ultimately spent on the research.

As with many conceptual models Figure 2.1 represents an idealised process but should serve as a basis for focusing the student's mind if difficulty is being experienced in selecting one or more promising topics. The following sections explore the implications of the various stages outlined.

APPOINTING THE SUPERVISOR

Most books on research methods pay little regard to the role of the supervisor in research studies. In part this is due to the fact that such books are addressed to all researchers, many of whom are solely accountable for the work they do. Almost by definition, however, any 'student' within a formalised education system must be complemented by a 'teacher'. In the particular context of student research activity the 'teacher' is usually referred to as the 'supervisor', although other descriptions such as project director, may be encountered. In this book 'supervisor' will be used to imply the individual to whom the student turns for regular guidance. It is, nevertheless, appreciated that many students will receive a minimum of supervision during their projects and this book will seek to fulful that role in these situations.

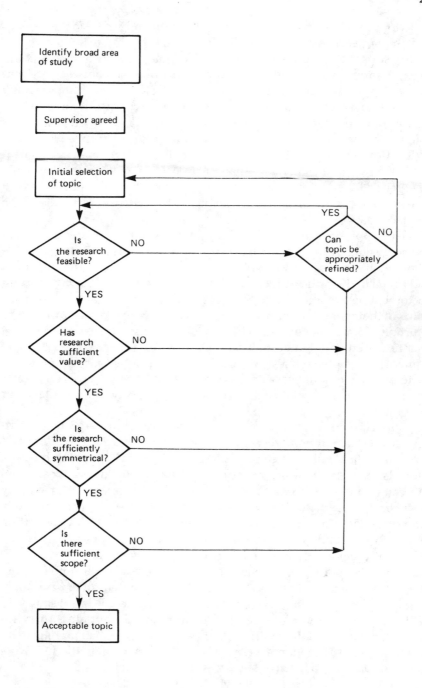

Figure 2.1   The process of topic selection

More is written in Chapter 7 on the relationship between the student and the supervisor. Comments in this chapter will be limited to the supervisor's role up to the point when the topic is finally agreed and the research proposal accepted. The extent of the dialogue between student and supervisor will normally be related to the level at which the research is being undertaken. Thus academic staff may have a list of topics which are appropriate for students below research degree level whereas research students are more likely to have a clearer idea as to what they would like to do. Although topic selection at research degree level may be an arduous process the likelihood is that the precise topic which eventually emerges will in large part have been identified by the student, and as such will provide an opportunity to establish an academic reputation in a specific area.

The 'apprentice model' in which a doctoral student relates directly to one, occasionally two, but rarely more, supervisor(s) throughout the whole of his project (with which he is concerned from the outset) is traditional in the British educational system. By contrast North American doctoral students attend taught courses for the first half or even two-thirds of their period of study before commencing their projects under the direction of a member of staff. This model has, in some areas of the social sciences, been adopted in the UK when the first year has been devoted primarily to taught courses. As efforts to increase the 'normal' period of doctoral study to four years have been resisted this has put even greater stress on the need for the effective management of the time available for the project.

Supervision, which may be weak in the case of undergraduate projects, should be strong at research degree level where both student and supervisor should share common interests. The problem of matching the interests of student and supervisor is a feature of the apprentice model and can result in a strong candidate being lost to research or equally unsatisfactorily, embarking upon a line of research to which he is not fully committed. A clear advantage of models of study which delay the setting up of a formal student/supervisor relationship is the opportunity which arises for 'breaking the ice' before commitment is made.

The opportunity cost of pursuing a research study full-time for from one to three years (that is the 'cost' of not doing what otherwise might have been done) may be very high if a successful outcome is not achieved. In this respect the importance of obtaining an appropriate supervisor cannot be overstated. It would be the first indication of bad management of their research if students were not to obtain answers to the following questions about prospective supervisors:

1. What is his record in terms of student completions?
2. What is his view of the management of student research and in particular his role in it?
3. How eminent is he in his specialism?
4. In addition to being knowledgeable about his subject has he high competence in research methodology?
5. How accessible is he?

Since individuals respond in different ways to the uncertainties of research, the student will need to base his decision, in part, on the type of relationship to which he responds best. Thus the highly creative, independent student might put most emphasis on 3 above, whereas a student who responds best to a fair degree of direction will probably place more weight on points 2 and 4.

If the student is intending to conduct his studies part-time he should recognise that supervisors will often feel less committed. Although, in the UK, the apprentice model will still normally apply, to an extent this is due to the greater duration of the research rendering the findings both remote and uncertain. Part-time study can be very demanding but can be much facilitated if the student is prepared to sustain a strong initiative in his dealings with his supervisor.

INITIAL SELECTION OF A TOPIC

It would be almost tautological to claim that the eventual successful completion of a research study will be seen to have depended on the selection of an appropriate topic. For each student however a range of possible topics will exist and some will prove to be more 'appropriate' than others. The possibility that a student who has been accepted by an institution should fail due to an inability to identify a topic is wholly inconsistent in the last resort with the responsibility which the institution has itself in this matter. Nevertheless the student, particularly at the higher levels, has a significant part to play in topic selection and it is our contention that by adopting a thorough and well ordered approach the chances of selecting a topic which will enhance completion prospects will be much improved. In what follows we are proposing a mechanism which should greatly assist in the identification of a line of study which will be consistent with the student's interests and abilities.

Figure 2.1 suggests that a logical sequence should be followed before a topic is finally selected. In practice the researcher will probably subject his ideas to the tests indicated without necessarily being aware that he is doing so in a particular order. Nevertheless before finally selecting a topic it should be rigorously exposed to the tests listed.

The first step is to identify areas which seem to have potential. The supervisor should of course be involved at this stage and may in fact have a ready-made topic which appeals to the student. If this is not the case the student must:

1. Identify an apparently novel topic;
2. Be able to convince himself and others of the novelty of the topic.

Requirement 1 implies a degree of creativity the extent of which will relate to the level at which the research is to be undertaken. Requirement 2 will involve a systematic search of the literature along the lines to be described in Chapter 4. It is customary to consider several topics during the selection process and it is sensible that the student should identify as many potentially rewarding lines as he can.

Only at the level of the research degree does it become necessary to add to the body of knowledge to any significant extent. Therefore at this level an early step must be to determine what the body of knowledge is. The supervisor has an obvious contribution to make at this stage.

There are numerous sources of ideas for research. It is assumed that the supervisor will discharge his responsibilities appropriately at this stage by being both proactive (putting forward his own suggestions) and reactive (responding to the student's findings).

Suggestions for research topics may arise from the following:

1. Theses and dissertations;
2. Articles in academic and professional journals;
3. Reports;
4. Books and book reviews;
5. Communication with experts in the field;
6. Conversations with potential users of the research findings;
7. Discussions with colleagues;
8. The media.

The level at which the research is undertaken will affect the extent to which the student uses the sources listed. The PhD student must expect to cover most if not all of them as it is vital for him to establish that his work is original. At other levels convenience and access are likely to dictate the action taken.

Sources 1 to 4 imply access to a high quality library; the quality being measured in terms of its stock of literature and, the ability of the library staff to procure texts from other libraries. In similar vein the local library staff should be able to suggest to the student which other libraries could be visited with advantage.

All theses, many dissertations and other student reports contain suggestions for additional research. Journal articles sometimes include recommendations for further work, and as they are normally reasonably up to date (appearing a year or so after the completion of a study) should be given appropriate attention by the researcher. Reports, particularly of government sponsored bodies, although often the outcome of protracted enquiries, are usually published with some speed. Again these often contain recommendations on which research can be based. Books give a detailed account of particular fields and consequently will figure prominently in a researcher's studies. They do nevertheless possess the disadvantage that they are not as up to date as the other written sources mentioned, and their contents may have become known to other researchers. It will be noted that source 4 includes book reviews as well as books. The reviewers of a book are usually able to evaluate the extent of its contribution to knowledge and can provide a useful service for students seeking ideas for topics. As no one has yet thought to produce bibliographies of reviews all that the researcher can do is to scan relevant publications which are known to contain reviews. The essential step of gaining access to relevant published material will be examined in depth in Chapter 4.

Sources 5 to 7 listed above require rather more initiative than does a search of the literature. The notion that research can be pursued from behind a desk may appeal to some students but whatever the field much advantage may be gained from discussions with others. Active researchers are usually sympathetic towards students who are undertaking studies in an area of mutual interest. Ideas for research can sometimes be tested during a brief conversation on the telephone or at conferences and seminars but ideally an appointment should be sought where potential topics can be discussed more fully. These comments apply with particular force to doctoral level students who are able to identify an individual from another institution or organisation who is obviously a leader in his field. In these circumstances a journey of some distance may well prove to be a highly useful investment. Although there will be some circularity in the sense that the nature of the research will not be defined until the topic has been selected the field in which the student is working will probably favour certain categories of research which might be linked to potential users. Thus a research student in bio-chemistry might make contact with the research departments of companies manufacturing fertilisers, or an engineering student could initiate discussions with a company making hydraulic valves.

Much may be gained when a few ideas have been formulated by discussing them informally with colleagues (students and staff). In this respect the advantage of working within a research group is obvious and the need for greater initiative on the part of the lone research student is highlighted.

The media should not be ignored as a potential source of topics. Researchers are disinclined to publish their findings until they have been sufficiently substantiated but newspapers, popular journals, and radio and television may report on research progress which is felt to be of general interest. Additionally, major findings may be reported by the media perhaps twelve months before scholarly accounts appear in learned journals. Students in the social sciences in particular may through awareness of the media, be able to identify issues within which research topics may be located.

TECHNIQUES FOR GENERATING RESEARCH TOPICS

Experience suggests that methods of evaluating topics and suggestions as to where to look for them are often ineffective. Students often need specific methods that will guide them in the topic selection process. These need to be capable of providing useful guidance for two very different types of student; the 'underfocused' whose ideas of subject area are not specific enough to form the basis of a viable thesis topic and the 'overfocused' who has a singleminded aim of pursuing a particular topic. The underfocused student needs ways of refining rather vague and often somewhat grandiose notions of a research area. The methods that are useful to him are those that enable him to identify a researchable 'niche' which he is capable of exploiting with the time and resources at his disposal. The overfocused student might seem by contrast to have the ideal attitude for successful research, but it must be remembered that research is a specialised business and that it is by no means unknown for students who have a clear idea of the research they wish to do to find that it has been done already, a fact of which they are unaware simply because of unfamiliarity with the frontiers of the subject. Where a supervisor has indicated an area for study this is less likely to be a problem but the implication of Figure 2.1 is that there are occasions when the best decision a student can make about a possible research topic is to drop it. For both types of student there is virtue in having methods that are capable of suggesting alternative themes given a starting subject. The techniques that are helpful in topic selection are essentially part of the field of 'creativity or problem solving theory'. Useful detailed discussions of these fields can be found, for instance, in books by Tarr (1973), de Bono (1976) and Ackoff (1978). Three approaches of considerable use to the researcher will be discussed here in more depth: the use of analogy, relevance trees and morphological analysis.

The Use of Analogy

Analogy plays an important role in many types of research. It aids the research process in two ways: it may suggest a fruitful line of enquiry in a particular subject area based on a perceived resemblance to some other area or it may suggest methods of analysis devised for use in one field which may profitably be employed in another. This latter role is exemplified by say statistical techniques and will be discussed further in Chapter 5. The use of analogy in topic formation is the principal interest here. As an example of this process take the case of the researcher with an interest in small business innovation who notes that many experts have suggested that the advanced equipment used in the West is inappropriate in developing countries and that the latter need 'intermediate technology' better suited to their less developed technical infrastructure. On reflection he perceives that the gap between the most advanced small businesses and the least is by no means dissimilar to that between the West and certain of the developing nations. From there it is a short step to speculate about 'intermediate technology' in the small business and the forms it might take (for example, in methods of information processing).

Relevance Trees

Though the name 'relevance trees' originated in the field of research and development management (c. f. Jantsch, 1967), their attraction is that they are excellent models of one of the ways people think about problems. Essentially a relevance tree suggests a way of developing related ideas from a starting concept. To be most effective the starting concept should be fairly broad. The relevance tree then serves as a device either for generating alternative topics or for fixing on some 'niche'. The importance of both functions has, of course, already been noted.

Figure 2.2 shows an example of a relevance tree. Starting from the broad area of 'Demand for transport' the researcher first identifies two major factors affecting it, 'Need to Travel' and 'Individuals' ability to afford travel', which in turn can be related to 'Incomes' and 'Cost of

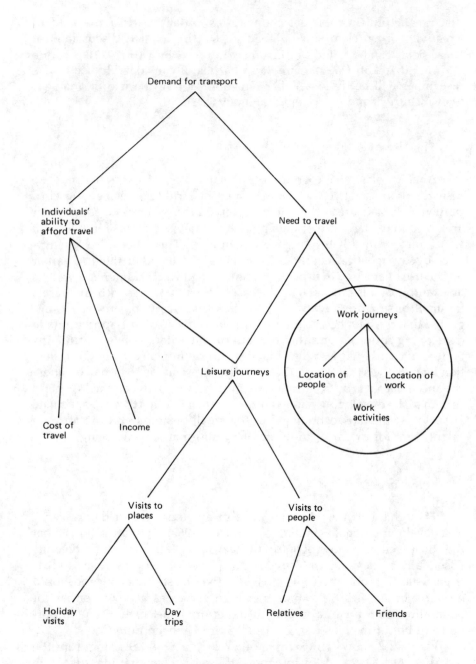

Figure 2.2   Example of a relevance tree

Types of management research project

Major factors

Aim	Design	Focus
Delineation	Historical analysis	Issue / activity
Explanation	Case study	Profession / interest group
Measurement	Testing of hypothesis	Several organisations
Classification	Comparative analysis	Single organisation
Variable / concept development	Conceptual models	Several departments
Technique development	Mathematical models	One department
Prediction		Several projects
Policy analysis		One project
Theory development		

Figure 2.3   Example of morphological analysis

travel'. The first factor he splits again into 'Leisure journeys' (also affected by the ability to afford travel) and into 'Work journeys'. Determinants of the latter factor are seen to be 'Location of work' (where it is carried out), 'Location of people' (where they live) and 'Work activities'. This last set of ringed variables might suggest to the researcher a possible topic, namely the extent to which changes in the forms of work activity will affect in the longer term where people live and how far and how frequently they travel to work.

Morphological Analysis

Morphological analysis (cf. Jantsch, 1967) is another technique originally developed for use in industrial research and development. Basically it relies upon a threefold process of:

a) defining the key factors or dimensions of a particular subject;
b) listing the various attributes of the factor or ways it can occur;
c) defining all feasible combinations of the attributes.

Figure 2.3 shows an example of morphological analysis for defining valid types of management research. It is supposed, for the purpose of illustration, that the body of knowledge to be used is already known but that it is desired to identify a topic of sufficient potential for doctoral research.

The researcher has selected three major factors defining type of management research:

Aim –   What it is for;
Design –   Which methodology is employed;
Focus –   The group activity which is to be researched.

Various possible attributes of each factor are now listed. Different types of research project can then be generated by taking one attribute from each of the three columns of Figure 2.3 for example:

Explanation – Comparative analysis – Several organisations which, clearly, would involve the researcher in attempting to explain some phenomenon by comparative analysis of data drawn from several organisations.

In practice not all combinations are feasible, for example, the limited scope for comparative analysis within one department. However, it will often be found that combinations involving two or more attributes of one or several factors are attractive, for example:

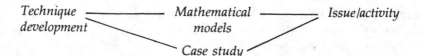

a design frequently encountered in practice because of the opportunity it gives for testing the performance of the techniques developed in an actual situation.

Morphological analysis is capable of generating a very large number of alternatives. For this reason it is necessary to define only a few key dimensions or factors and to restrict the aspects of each that are considered. This forces the user to structure his problem and is thus particularly useful to the underfocused student who finds it difficult to get to grips with topic selection.

FEASIBILITY OF THE RESEARCH PROPOSED

There is little purpose in attempting a full evaluation of a topic unless the research to which it leads is feasible. The student should therefore consider the following factors:

1. availability of and access to data and information;
2. opportunity to pursue a particular research design;
3. the time needed to complete the research;
4. the technical skills needed by him;
5. financial support;
6. the risk involved.

The six factors may be relevant to all levels of research and the first two can be insurmountable obstacles.

1. Access and Availability

The first factor may be exemplified by a student who has selected as a research topic the variation in manufacturing costs in different countries within multinational car firms. Some car companies may be prepared to state in which countries costs are particularly high but it is unlikely that sufficient if any would disclose detailed data. This may be an obvious example but students should satisfy themselves that there is reasonable prospect of access before proceeding further. A more difficult assessment for the student to make at this stage is whether data or information which will be essential to the research actually exist. Clearly, planned approaches involving the analysis of secondary data (which are not gathered by the researcher) will be impossible if the data have not been recorded or are unreliable.

2. Opportunity for Research Design

The student may be inclined towards a topic in which a laboratory features and in many cases such researchers will be able to set up experiments in their own institution's laboratories. If however the student intends to conduct a field experiment some degree of co-operation will normally be needed. For example, pricing policy for academic journals may well be felt to be a suitable topic for research, but it would be unlikely that a publisher could be found who would agree to handing over control of pricing to a student. Similar difficulties may be encountered in attempts to arrange a survey. Thus a researcher may wish to study member/officer relationships within a particular local authority. Before proceeding further he must satisfy himself that he will be allowed to approach the subjects of his investigation. To attempt to proceed without approval is likely to lead to complete frustration of his plans.

3. Time Available

A prime aim of this book is to assist students to complete their research within the time available to them. In some instances research is designed without proper thought being given to the time needed for its completion. For example the development of an anti-corrosive paint could be an appropriate outcome of a research study, but the time required to assess the anti-corrosive properties added to the development period may far exceed the time available to a student researcher. Another question is whether too much is being attempted within the time available for research. When the topic has been selected much is to be gained by drawing up a research plan which will indicate whether the deadlines can be met.

4. Technical Skills

It is reasonable to assume that student research at any level is more likely to succeed if the topic chosen will utilise skills and knowledge already possessed. There would for example seem to be greater prospects of satisfactory completion if a student with a first degree in physics were to research in this subject rather than in botany. In some instances, however, it is impossible to avoid having to acquire new skills if a topic is to be researched effectively. This is particularly so in the social sciences where skills often require to be developed in statistics, mathematics, and computing. A student should therefore consider very carefully whether the topic he has chosen matches the skills he possesses or will have time to develop during the course of his study. If doubt exists the supervisor should be able to give guidance.

5. Financial Support

Much research has foundered because of a lack of resources. In student research where the prime resource is the individual concerned it is usual for the financial support needed for the study to have been resolved before work is started. The student's budget will include funds to support normal research expenditure which may involve travelling, purchase of books, cost of typing and so on. Many students are, however, unclear as to what expenditure will be covered by their sponsor (for some details of support for student research see Turner, 1978) but this is unlikely to cover the purchase of expensive equipment or materials, or unlimited travel and subsistence and may not extend to postal questionnaires. Before a topic is finally selected therefore the question of cost must be examined. Inability to undertake certain activities due to a shortage of funds may prejudice a potentially successful study if the problem is not anticipated and resolved at the outset.

6. The Risk Involved

As a final point the student should consider the risk that the project will take much longer than expected or even prove impossible to complete. It will be remembered that in discussing the nature of research in Chapter 1 the point was made that some types of research are perhaps inherently more risky than others and the student should, therefore, at least decide whether the risk of the project he proposes is acceptable to him.

The above comments have been made particularly with full-time research in mind. They apply with even greater force to part-time researchers with the one exception that in longitudinal studies involving an evaluation of some phenomenon over time the part-timer may have an advantage because of the longer duration of his study. In the UK, for example, most degree awarding bodies although preferring a part-time doctorate to be completed within about seven years would be tolerant towards a student registration of up to a decade providing evidence of progress could be given. Social, economic, or political 'experiments' often need lengthy periods of evaluation, and as such would exceed the two or three years available to full-time research students.

No apology is made if the observations appear to be somewhat negative. By giving systematic consideration to the feasibility of the topic and the risks it entails the student will be forced to think carefully about the purpose of the research and the approach he will adopt. If the topic can satisfy the demands of feasibility as described the student will be well equipped to complete the planning phase (see Figure 1.2); if not the prospect of a future disaster can be avoided by refining the topic or selecting another.

VALUE OF THE RESEARCH

Having satisfied himself that the topic is feasible the student next needs to consider whether it has sufficient value. In some respects the student is in a privileged position in that the value of research may be judged purely on epistemological grounds with no ready prospect of the findings doing other than adding to the body of knowledge in a field. At the level of the undergraduate or the post-graduate dissertation the question of value may be resolved even more easily as the prime aim is to demonstrate a measure of research competence or problem solving ability (through for example a literature search or a case study).

The right of researchers to select topics which have no apparent value for the community at large is however being increasingly questioned. For example evidence was given in May 1980 by the UK Social Science Research Council (SSRC) (which gives much support for students reading for postgraduate degrees by study and dissertation or by research alone) to the House of Commons Committee of Public Accounts (1980 pp. 20–1). Some of the comments of committee members focused on the apparent lack of value of research supported by the SSRC either because it seemed to have little relevance to the United Kingdom or because it was difficult to understand how the results could be implemented practically. The SSRC in its turn appeared to accept that in general publicly funded research should be of potential value to the nation but pointed out that support is given for 'research of this type for some minimum level of activity in every civilised country'.

There is little point in studying apparently irrelevant and trivial topics if alternative topics of 'importance' can be identified. A further advantage of working on a topic of some significance is that the student is much more likely to be motivated; a frame of mind essential for successful completion. In addition both the supervisor (and ultimately any external examiner) is likely to take a greater interest if the research outcome is of undoubted value. The student who elects to pursue a topic that has little obvious value must expect in today's research climate that this aspect of the research will at examination receive much more attention than hitherto.

It is of course indicative of a thorough approach to a study if the student is convinced that a topic of value has been identified. In realising this situation advice will normally have been taken from experts in the area in addition to the supervisor. The model depicted in Figure 2.1 is, however, an idealised one and it is possible that changes made to the topic for one reason (for example, infeasibility) may fundamentally alter its ability to satisfy other requirements (for example, value). For example it may have been agreed initially by a doctoral student and his supervisor that the research would focus on the relationship between education authorities in England and central government. The student after considering the extent of the fieldwork involved may have decided that he would prefer to examine the relationship between one education authority only and central government. Although studies in depth have their own attractions and advantages value would probably be lost because of the restricted scope for generalisation afforded by a single case study. In order to avoid such an eventuality it is evident that second opinions should be sought at each new stage or redirection.

There is unfortunately no easy way to measure the value of research, and indeed its importance in student research is related to the level of the activity, being much more important in the case of doctoral studies. The best advice to students is probably for them to continue to search for an alternative topic if the one under consideration seems to be of doubtful value.

RESEARCH SYMMETRY

Figure 2.1 suggests that even though a student may be satisfied that research is both feasible and potentially valuable there are still two stages of an idealised process to go through before a topic is finally selected. The first of these requires that the alternative outcomes of the study should be identified. Although below research degree level there may be only one outcome, for example, the writing up of a literature search or a case study, in more advanced research two or more outcomes may be possible – a hypothesis may be proved, disproved, or an experiment may provide a definite result or may be inconclusive. Preferably each of the outcomes should represent acceptable findings in which case the risk involved in the research will be reduced.

The extent to which the outcomes are of similar value is an indication of the symmetry of the research. The student should seek to select a topic which promises high symmetry, but the prospects will be affected by the research approach which is adopted. Thus some research work of an experimental nature undertaken in laboratories by scientists and engineers may be highly asymmetrical and may ultimately fail to achieve a positive result. Alternatively a student may be unable to validate an econometric model which he has developed, perhaps mainly from theory. In both of these instances this would lead to there being no basis for the award of a research degree.

Symmetry depends in large part, on prior beliefs about a topic which are held within a field of study. If, for example, there is strong support for the view that the eating of sweets damages children's teeth or there is little belief that the phases of the moon affect work output, experiments which confirm strongly held opinion will not be rated highly even though the design and conduct of the experiments could not be criticised. Obviously if the research findings were to contradict current belief they would be of potential value but this is unlikely in both cases cited. An example of the symmetrical research topic would be one concerned with the effect on career progress of students who attain the degree of Master in Business Administration (MBA). If it were found that the MBA had no effect on career progress this conclusion would be of considerable value as would the contrary finding (although note should be taken of 'scope' as discussed in the next section).

One possible outcome of research is that the findings are inconclusive. The student should satisfy himself that the probability of this type of outcome is sufficiently low. As an example consider a topic in which a student is seeking to establish whether a theory of leadership based on research into a number of companies in the private sector is applicable also to management in the public sector. If a hypothesis to this effect were to be proved or disproved either finding could be of considerable value. Although the topic may be symmetrical with regard to conclusive outcomes the student may feel that there is a distinct possibility of an inconclusive outcome and that this makes the research insufficiently symmetrical to pursue.

It is evident that symmetry is to be preferred if the research lends itself to it. In this way research which satisfies all other criteria should lead to a successful outcome. It is not wished, however, to imply that success or failure always involves symmetry. Research which is of an exploratory or descriptive nature will normally have only one outcome which will be assessed at some point on a scale ranging from unacceptable to acceptable.

SCOPE FOR RESEARCH

The final test of a research topic as suggested in Figure 2.1 is that of assessing whether sufficient scope exists. In large part scope will be related to work already completed in related areas. As a result of such work prior beliefs will be held and these will affect the reaction to the research outcome in terms of novelty and surprise. Prior beliefs may range from virtual certainty (for example, that the earth moves round the sun) to complete uncertainty (for example, whether life exists elsewhere in the universe). Scope should be seen as the opportunity to increase, reduce, or even confirm (if these are based on analogies) current beliefs.

In considering scope the student should reflect also on the value of his potential topic. If this is high there may be sufficient scope even if prior beliefs are strongly held (for example in the case of the effect of smoking on health). It goes without saying that findings which overturn strongly held beliefs on matters of importance will be rated highly but these opportunities will present themselves rarely to the student researcher. The topics to be avoided are those which are potentially low in both surprise and value (here in the broadest epistemological sense). Thus a researcher might select as a topic the speed of learning of a foreign language by child expatriates. It would come as no surprise and would be of little apparent value to find that British children in families living in France or Germany gain a more rapid command of the languages of these countries than do their counterparts living in the UK. On the other hand there may be both surprise and value in finding that the same children demonstrate higher competence in mathematics than do children of similar ages in the UK. Though the standards required vary from one level of research to another the student should satisfy himself that the topic has sufficient potential along the dimensions of both scope and value.

DEVELOPING A RESEARCH PROPOSAL

At all levels of study considerable benefit can be gained by systematic planning. Figure 2.1 represents a process in which many of the answers to questions raised will be vague and unco-ordinated; probably being held within the mind of the researcher. The aim must be to develop a realistic plan of action with clear objectives which, taking account of resources and constraints, has a high probability of being achieved. The planning process itself is discussed in the next chapter but at this point reference is made to certain documents which the student should be prepared to compile: the topic analyses and the research proposal.

It is recommended that research degree students should undertake preparation of both documents. At other levels the proposal alone will normally suffice. Topic analyses and the research proposal will contribute to the achievement of the first major milestone; namely when both supervisor and student have agreed the study to be pursued.

Experience shows that the step of submitting views in writing for consideration by supervisors and others can be highly beneficial for

Section	Topic analyses (2 or 3 pages)	Research proposal (10 to 15 pages)
Summary	–	X
Hypothesis or research objective	X	X
Prior research in the area	X	X
Value in terms of the possible outcomes	X	X
Probable methodology or approach to the research	X	X
Tentative schedule	–	X
Provisional chapter details	–	X

Table 2.1   Content of topic analyses and the research proposal

students. Redirection of research can be accommodated much more readily at earlier rather than later stages and yet some students are reluctant to commit themselves to paper.

Both the topic analyses and the research proposal are of similar structure and the latter is in fact an elaborated version of a topic analysis. The sections of each are shown in Table 2.1

The Topic Analysis

Topic analyses are convenient ways of summarising various aspects of one or more potentially acceptable topics. A topic analysis should not exceed two or three pages in length and should contain summaries following careful consideration of each of the sections of Table 2.1 rather than a set of speculative observations.

One factor which causes some students much concern in the early stages of their research is the *hypothesis*. Simon, 1968, p. 37 defines a hypothesis as 'a single statement that attempts to explain or to predict a single phenomenon' (as opposed to a *theory* which is an entire system of interrelated thought). If a novel hypothesis can be substantiated there will be an addition to the body of knowledge and hence the attraction to the researcher of identifying an appropriate hypothesis. In many instances however the purpose of the research does not lend itself to other than trivial hypotheses. Thus a chemist may hypothesise that a single dye can be developed which will provide an immediate camouflage effect but this would be stated much more sensibly as a research objective. There is no reason why more than one hypothesis should not be formulated. Thus a study of innovation might incorporate hypotheses on the size of organisations and the managerial style of R and D departments. In general however it is preferable to avoid too detailed a specification of the research. It is usually better to identify a single hypothesis with considerable potential for testing.

The section of the topic analysis dealing with research value will be highly significant when research degrees are involved and will encompass the comments made above on intrinsic value, symmetry and scope of the research. It will be strengthened if evidence can be provided that authorities in the field agree that there is a need for the research proposed.

If more than one topic proves to be acceptable to both a student and his supervisor the final choice will most probably depend upon the weightings attached by the student to the value of the research and the approach likely to be adopted. Some students react positively to the challenge of higher value (but often higher risk) studies whereas others wish to maximise the chances of completing their research and hence select the topic most consistent with this aim.

Those students for whom the completion of a topic analysis is an essential part of the planning phase may wish to model their approach on the example which is presented at Appendix 1.

The Research Proposal

Whereas a topic analysis should contain just sufficient information for a decision to be reached on the line of research to be pursued the research proposal should be seen as the document which finally establishes the need for the study and that the researcher has or can acquire the skills and other resources required. The student should in fact imagine that he is tendering for a research contract through the medium of the research proposal. In reality it is highly probable that the latter will need to be refined, possibly more than once.

The final version of the proposal might be 10 to 15 pages in length. In those sections which are common to both the topic analysis and the research proposal the main elaboration in the latter case will be on prior research and probable methodology. The student will accumulate many additional references during the course of his research and writing but before he embarks on the execution phase he must be able to satisfy himself and his advisers that he is wholly familiar with previous and current work in the area of his planned study. In addition to guaranteeing novelty this will be a major factor in assessing the value of possible outcomes. Thus the accout of prior research as indicated by the list of references and the bibliography contained within the research proposal should be comprehensive.

The proposal will need to describe in sufficient detail the approach which the student will use. In large measure this will indicate whether or not the line of study planned is feasible. The five factors identified in the section 'Feasibility of the research proposed' should be addressed in the proposal. Thus descriptions will need to be given of such matters as the sampling frame and method, type of equipment needed, the data to be collected, the nature of the experiment, and the methods of analysis to be employed. This will probably be the most difficult section of the research proposal to write and there should be much resort to expert advice. Inevitably there will be questions still to be resolved. The student must however, ask himself the question 'Dare I risk proceeding when uncertainty remains?'. In some instances the answer must be 'no'. It would, for example, be ridiculous to write up a proposal which did not guarantee the opportunity to pursue a particular research design. On the other hand it would be reasonable for a student who is familiar with one computer programming language to assume that he could acquire skills in another.

Although only tentative it is desirable that a schedule should be incorporated in a research proposal. With limited time at his disposal it is important that a student should become used to thinking in terms of deadlines. Such a schedule will be beneficial to the student when he commences to draw up his research plan.

Similarly much is to be gained by including within the research proposal details of the chapters which will appear in the written account. Most of these accord with a standard and logical structure, an example (Howard, 1978) which relates to doctoral theses is as follows:

1. The introduction describing the general problem area, the specific problem, why the topic is important, prior research, approach of the thesis, limitations and key assumptions, and contribution to be made by the research.
2. A description of what has been done in the past. This is a complete survey of prior research which if very nominal, might be combined with chapter 1. If there is extensive prior research, the results might preferably be broken down into two or more chapters. It is normally an important section of the thesis because the description of what has been done provides background and also documents the fact that the candidate's research is unique as the thesis is not duplicating earlier work.
3. A description of the research methodology. One or more chapters may be used to describe the research method. For example, the chapter(s) might describe a simulation model, a data collection technique, a measurement technique, an experiment, or an historical method of analysis. In essence, this section describes how the research was conducted.
4. The research results. The results of the chosen methodology are reported: the data are presented, the conceptual framework is described, the historical analysis is defined, or the comparative studies are explained.
5. Analysis of the results. This may be included with earlier chapters depending upon the type of thesis. This is a key section because it explains the conclusions that can be drawn from the data, the implications of a theory and so on.
6. Summary and conclusions. The thesis is summarised with emphasis upon the results obtained and the contribution made by these results. Any suggestions for further research are also outlined.

The purpose of a research proposal should not be forgotten. It should not be seen as a progress report to be filed but as a document for decision. Although the supervisor should be encouraging the student to submit the proposal the decision to be taken is of sufficient importance for the student himself to take the initiative in arranging a meeting which will be attended by advisers other than the supervisor. The result of this meeting should be general agreement that the researcher should now be able to proceed with some confidence. If such agreement does not materialise it is to be hoped that sufficient constructive criticism will have been obtained for a revised proposal to have a good chance of acceptance on the next round.

SUMMARY

TOPIC SELECTION: is a process which can absorb a
significant proportion of a research study. Certain steps can,
however, be recognised which enable a systematic approach
towards topic selection to be adopted; this should reduce the
probability of excessive time being spent on this stage.

AN APPROPRIATE SUPERVISOR: should be appointed as
soon as possible and should be heavily involved during the
topic selection process.

THE GENERATION OF RESEARCH TOPICS: may be
facilitated by a number of techniques which include analogy,
relevance trees and morphological analysis.

THE ACCEPTABILITY OF A RESEARCH TOPIC: may be
judged by giving consideration to its feasibility, value,
symmetry, and scope.

A RESEARCH PROPOSAL: should be developed when a
topic has been provisionally agreed so that the full
implications of the study will emerge from detailed planning.

Planning the Research Project

THE NEED TO PLAN THE RESEARCH PROJECT

There are a number of reasons why students experience difficulty in research. The most important of these are firstly difficulties in selecting a suitable topic; secondly, the problem of selecting an appropriate analytical framework, and thirdly, inability to manage available resources, in particular their time. The third reason is common at all levels of research, and is often symptomatic of the previous two. Where students have problems in planning content these often reflect themselves in wasted time and lack of progress.

The aim of this chapter is accordingly very simple. It is to present the student with a tool for planning his own research project which will

enable him to realise when he has run into serious difficulties. More importantly perhaps it is intended to function as a motivational device by enabling him to see that he is achieving goals he has set himself, since experience shows that the best way to successful completion of the research as a whole is through acquiring the habit of successful completion of intermediate stages.

Although the type of planning to be described is in itself a useful process through which desirable courses of action are identified, and potential pitfalls are anticipated, a major justification is that it serves as a basis for control. What is required is not a loose collection of estimates of what the research will involve but a comprehensively analysed schedule of activities against which research progress may be assessed. The planning referred to in this chapter is not that concerned with the nature of the research itself; for example, the approach adopted towards setting up an experiment in a hospital or towards a special literature search. Rather it is concerned with the management of the research project which will be seen as a number of distinct but interrelated stages or activities all of which must be completed before the study is finished. Although the activities will differ in importance each will be planned to the same degree to indicate when, ideally, they should take place.

The major purposes of such planning are:

a) to clarify the aims and objectives of the researcher;
b) to define the activities required to attain these aims and the order in which they take place;
c) to identify various critical points or 'milestones' in the research at which progress can be reviewed and the research plan reassessed;
d) to produce estimates of times at which the various milestones will be reached so that progress can be clearly measured;
e) to ensure that effective use is made of key resources particularly the researcher himself;
f) to define priorities once the research is underway;
g) to serve as a guide for increasing the likelihood of successful completion on time.

If this list seems needlessly elaborate and more relevant to the construction of, say, a motorway bridge than the conduct of a student research project, the reader should remember that the fewer the resources of time and money the greater the need for careful planning and that in any research project the key resource is always his own time. Furthermore planning is most necessary where the activities involved are non-routine so that possible difficulties can be anticipated.

A major difference between the planning of research and the construction of a bridge is that in the former case the work content of the various stages cannot always be readily estimated. It is presumed however that students will have selected a topic which can be researched within the time available and that although original work and deadlines conflict to some extent, the implied time constraints will be accepted.

NETWORK PLANNING

A planning approach should be adopted which will serve as a basis for control of projects of various lengths but will be sufficiently flexible to accommodate the unpredictabilities of research. Given the success of network analysis techniques in planning and controlling industrial research projects as well as complex construction programmes some form of network is indicated.

The development of the computer in the 1950s stimulated the application of network analysis particularly to construction projects in which thousands of activities may be involved. Much has subsequently been written about techniques of network analysis (see for example, Lockyer, 1969). Their primary purpose is to assist in planning and control in situations in which the mind is unable to cope efficiently with the relationships among the numerous acitivities. The principles involved can be comprehended within an hour or two and application of the technique can be very beneficial to the completion of the study within the time available.

Thus though the procedures outlined are rather formal they can be applied by students at any level. As elsewhere, it is argued that research students should employ them unless either they are sufficiently experienced in managing research projects to have their own system (which will inevitably be fairly similar), or they agree with their supervisor that these methods are inappropriate in their case. Nevertheless the methods have value in their own right as a model of the major aspects of the process of planning a research project and may be so regarded, if desired.

It is felt that although the number of activities which can be identified in a student research project will usually be a few dozen at the most, network methods should be used to plan and control any project expected to last more than a few weeks. It may be that in some projects use could be made of one of the smaller network packages to be found on mini and micro computers to which many research students will have access. Providing, however, the number of activities to be incorporated in the network does not exceed the fifty or sixty manual control will be possible and may be preferred.

It should be appreciated that whatever the number of activities the network itself must be drawn by hand; the computer undertakes the analysis which leads to an indication of the start and finish times of activities and any spare time which exists.

AN EXAMPLE OF A NETWORK IN PLANNING STUDENT RESEARCH

In this section a hypothetical example will be employed drawing upon the research approach used by many students in the social sciences, namely the analysis of response to questionnaire based survey in order to test a hypothesis.

Nevertheless, whatever the level of research and whatever stage has been reached the process of network planning is always the same:

1. Determine the objectives.
2. Identify and list (in any order) the activities that need to be carried out.
3. Order the activities. Establish for every activity those activities which precede it, those which follow it, and those which may be undertaken concurrently.
4. Draw the network.
5. Estimate the time needed to complete each activity.
6. Analyse the network using the completion times.
7. Check the resources and draw up the schedule.
8. Replan as necessary.

1. Determine the objectives

As a first step the student should always review his objectives, since these may well influence many of the activities that appear in the list. In this case it is assumed that the student's primary objective is to pursue a career in social science research and that as a consequence he has defined during the first six months of his studies his subsidiary aims, that is to

a) work in an area with considerable research potential;

b) acquire familiarity with certain basic tools of social science research such as the conduct of surveys and the role of statistics in survey analysis, and the use of the computer for processing survey data;

c) successfully complete a PhD thesis in the $2\frac{1}{2}$ years (130 weeks) that he expects to remain a full-time student.

Obviously the points under b) are reflected in the number of activities on the list, whereas the requirement c) may well necessitate replanning if for some reason the analysis shows that the target cannot be met.

2. Listing Activities

The student will next need to decide the level at which the activities should be listed. This depends on the length of the project and the stage which has been reached. In a research project for a taught master's course, there will usually be little difficulty in producing a list of activities at the level of detail of Table 3.1 which will probably suffice for the whole project. Indeed students involved in projects as short as this are cautioned that, if they experience difficulties in drawing up a list of the activities or in assessing the time they will take, it may well mean that the project involves too much uncertainty and needs redefinition.

At the doctoral level however, it will normally be necessary to go through the planning process many times during the project and the level of detail appropriate at the beginning may be very different from that needed once a topic has been selected and the research is well underway. Thus at the very beginning a list of activities such as:

i)   attend Professor Brown's lectures;
ii) participate in FORTRAN for beginners course;
iii) select topic;
iv) draw up research proposal;
v)   carry out research

could well be quite adequate, in that it can serve as a basis for monitoring progress in the earlier stages, whilst not pretending to knowledge that the student does not have prior to topic selection.

Equally a slightly more complex model could be achieved by suitably adapting the stages of the research project shown in Figure 1.2. This would for example bring into some relief the time which could reasonably be allotted to the selection of the topic itself. In the present case however it is assumed that a research proposal has been submitted and accepted.

Activity number	Activity description	Estimated duration (weeks)
1.	Written statement of concepts and theories	3
2.	First draft of questionnaire for pilot study	6
3.	Finalising of questionnaire for pilot study	1
4.	Decide likely method of analysing response to survey	4
5.	Select participants for pilot study	4
6.	Acquire statistical skills	8
7.	Attend course on use of standard computer package	6
8.	Write drafts of early thesis chapters (three say)	9
9.	Carry out pilot study	4
10.	Review pilot study	3
11.	Prepare questionnaire for survey	4
12.	Decide target population and sampling details	4
13.	Carry out survey	12
14.	Process data for computer	6
15.	Interpret computer output	6
16.	Evaluate nature and extent of response to survey	4
17.	Write paper for presentation at conference	4
18.	Relate findings to concepts / theories / hypothesis	6
19.	Decide and carry out any further analysis or research	12
20.	Complete writing of draft chapters (five say)	15
21.	Review and edit thesis	10
22.	Correct thesis and obtain bound copies	4
23.	Prepare for oral examination	2
24.	Allowance for holidays, job interviews, illness and general contingencies	24

Table 3.1   A list of activities for a student research project in the social science field

Several activities that have already taken place, for example topic selection, do not, therefore, appear in the network. Planning is about what has to be done and not about what has been done.

It should be noted that the activities listed in Table 3.1 are typical in that they involve a mix of motivational activities, for example Write paper for presentation at conference; preparatory activities, for example Acquiring statistical skills; activities specific to the research project, for example, Carry out survey; and finally those required for reasons of health and sanity and not directly related to the work itself, for example Allowance for holidays. As far as the latter is concerned there is an element of flexibility in that it is part of the contingency allowance that is added to any time estimate. Thus in this case the student has not scheduled any summer holiday during the research project proper, preferring to improve his motivation to beat his schedule by earmarking some part of any time-savings he may make for holiday purposes.

It is sometimes the case that by slightly redefining the activity the student may considerably reduce the risk that his research will run into major problems. Thus here the student though anticipating a high response rate in his survey might well decide to despatch it to a much larger sample in case the response was far lower and in addition to incorporate certain features in the questionnaire to enable him to check for any bias in the eventual replies. Neither of these decisions is likely to have much effect on the time required for the activities they affect. On the other hand either or both of them considerably reduce the risk of failure through insufficient returns or returns with a serious but unrecognised bias.

As the research progresses and activities are completed, replanning may well necessitate changes to the list. Some activities may be dropped, but more likely, some will be broken down into finer detail as the relevant stage of the project approaches, for example Review and edit thesis might be expanded to include Get figures and tables produced; Review and correct Chapter 1; Review and correct Chapter 2 and so on.

Obviously this is only necessary for activities that are about to be undertaken and even then only if they involve the co-ordination of several interlinked, lesser activities. The expansion process is compensated for by the completion of earlier activities so that the list is never much longer than shown here. Alternatively it is possible to run two networks, a broad brush master network for the project as a whole and, where circumstances warrant it, a sub-network that breaks down a single master network activity into far finer detail, for example where the analysis stage necessitates a set of interrelated computer runs.

3. Order the Activities

The basic method used for drawing the network is to represent the activities by arrows and the order in which activities must take place by the ordering of the arrows. Thus the diagram

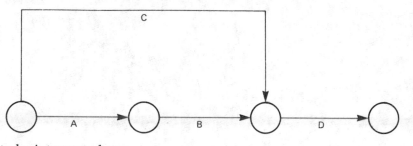

is to be interpreted as:

Activity A precedes Activity B;
Activity A must be completed before Activity B can start;
Activity C must be completed before Activity D can start;
Activity B must be completed before Activity D can start and Activities A and C can start at the same time.

Circles indicate the start/end of activities and are referred to as 'events'.

4. Draw the Network

The network of a research study represented at this level of detail can be drawn very quickly (see for example, Lockyer (1969) for further details). The outcome is depicted in Figure 3.1 after consideration has been given to the ordering of activities. The broken line in the network is referred to as a 'dummy' and is needed to indicate that certain activities (in this case those numbered 2, 5, 8, and 12) cannot commence until one or more preceding activities have been completed (in this case activity number 4).

The virtue of such a presentation is that the interrelationship between activities can be clearly seen, in particular, where the need for one activity to precede another is not immediately obvious. Furthermore the first few times this approach is used it may well remind the researcher of activities that have been overlooked. Points in the project at which in principle at least the student can be working on several activities at once are indicated by parallel paths through the network, for example Carry out pilot study and Decide target population and sampling details, and

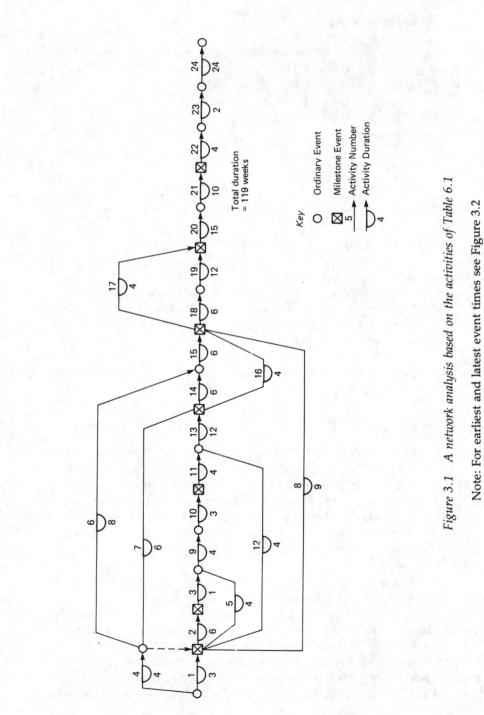

Figure 3.1   A network analysis based on the activities of Table 6.1

Note: For earliest and latest event times see Figure 3.2

Total duration
= 119 weeks

Key

◯   Ordinary Event

⊠   Milestone Event

5   Activity Number

4   Activity Duration

these may well be helpful in fitting his project schedule to the resources available. In short the diagram of Figure 3.1 shows the 'logic' of the project on which planning must be based and is of very considerable value in itself.

In fact some researchers use networks solely to indicate the way in which the project activities interact. One researcher, known to the authors for example, is usually involved in several projects which he records in a single large network and updates monthly because 'it is the only way I can keep track of what I am doing'.

The length of the arrows in the network is not related to the duration of the activity. It is, however, customary to indicate the passage of time by ensuring that all arrows point in a forward direction. So far no reference has been made to activity duration as much value can be gained by drawing the network and thus appreciating the order in which work should be done and, of much potential importance, reducing the probability of overlooking an important stage of the research. There is of course no certainty that the study will in execution correspond exactly with the structure of the network, but it should represent the views of the student at the current stage of the research project. Thus in Figure 3.1 activity number 19 ('Decide and carry out any further analysis or research') might be viewed at the time the network was drawn more as a contingency but in the event may involve several additional stages which need to be carefully planned.

5. Estimate Activity Times

A major advantage of the network approach is that by undertaking simple calculations a schedule of activities may be prepared and used for controlling the project. Included in Table 3.1 is an estimate of the number of weeks required to complete each of the twenty-four activities. It should be noted that 'Estimated duration' is the 'elapsed time', that is the time required to complete the activity. Usually this will be longer than the number of weeks of work entailed by the activity, because, say, the activity involves contacting individuals who are not immediately accessible or, more importantly, when time is needed to absorb information that has been gained and to integrate this into the researcher's conceptual framework. The task of estimation is not an easy one and the student will need advice from his supervisor and ideally from other students who have completed research in similar areas. Thus in the hypothetical example it may be possible to identify a researcher who has completed a questionnaire based survey which has considerable similarities to the study envisaged. His experiences would then be translated to assist in estimating the duration of activities 2, 3, 9, 10, 11 and 13 of Table 3.1. The student also, may be reasonably confident in estimating the time he will allocate to activities, 1, 5, 12, 17, 20, 21, 22 and 23. It is always necessary (particularly when thinking in terms of a specific individual) to recognise that account must be taken of activities such as holidays and illness which will not further the project work. These are included in activity 24 which it will be seen extends the duration of the project by about 20 per cent. Although, as we have said, allowances need to be built into each activity it is sensible that further latitude is provided to cover activities which are not related to the project.

This leaves activities, 4, 6, 7, 8, 14, 15, 16, 18 and 19 which can be roughly apportioned between two groups:

a) those for which the work content may be reasonably estimated but which are undertaken intermittently (activities 7 and 8);
b) those for which there is considerably uncertainty about the work content (activities 4, 6, 14, 15, 16, 18 and 19).

The estimating problem raised by group (a) is not too difficult to accommodate. A realistic minimum elapsed time equal to the content of the work should first be assigned to the activity. If after analysis the activity is found to be critical the student will need to establish whether parallel activities are involved and if so the extent to which the total period of the research must be extended. If the activity does not turn out to be critical there will then be scope for stretching it out over a longer period without jeopardising the completion of the project.

The preparation of schedules is made more difficult by the need to accommodate group (b) type activities which by definition are incapable of precise estimation. A further complication is the recognition that in some instances the work will be carried out intermittently. Indeed in the example only activity 19 (decisions on further analysis) will continuously occupy the student's attention. The problem may best be resolved by the student attempting to incorporate work content within 'elapsed time'. Thus activity 6 (acquisition of statistical skills) will require that the student should read certain texts but in order to ensure that the concepts are fully understood he may allocate an elapsed time of eight weeks (as used in Table 3.1) for the comprehension of issues arising from an estimated fifty hours of reading (a standard time of ten hours is sometimes used for each book read). In the example used activity 7 (attend course on standard computer package) is placed in group (a) as it is not envisaged that the student would need to gain competence in programming. If this were the case the activity would have been more appropriately placed in the group (b) category.

A number of general points apply to estimating activity times. Firstly, standard times exist for many unlikely tasks, for example reading books as cited above. Secondly, the student can often reduce the time he requires to carry out certain activities and incidentally improve his ability to estimate it by training/preparation, for instance by taking a rapid reading course before embarking on his literature search. Thirdly, allowances may need to be built in to all activity times to cope with the unexpected occurrences that always seem far more likely to extend the time required rather than reduce it. The need to do this can only be established in the light of the student's own performance on estimating. For this reason for all except the short research project it is recommended that the student records on a control chart (see Figure 3.3) how long activities actually take as compared with his initial estimate. During the course of the longer research project he can then hope to derive a realistic 'correction factor' to apply to his own first guesses. Though apparently naive this can be surprisingly effective.

The difficulty of handling uncertainty is probably the major problem in planning. In general (as in Table 3.1) single figure estimates are employed and give a spurious indication of likely accuracy but in some instances the ensuing errors of estimation are so great that the outcome of the project is prejudiced. An early application of the network approach which gained a considerable measure of publicity was to the Polaris programme of the US Navy. The network technique employed was described as PERT (Programme Evaluation and Review Technique) in which pessimistic, most likely, and optimistic estimates were made of durations. In this way, in addition to expected project completion times, it became possible to place probabilities upon particular events being completed by a certain date. It is not suggested that the student should go to this length but even if he were to the total time taken in this aspect of planning would still be only a very small part of the total study. Some students having come to appreciate the benefits of the approach may well be inclined to go as far as they can in order to provide the most effective basis for the control of their study, particularly if it is decided to use a computer package that incorporates the PERT facility.

6. Analyse the Network using the Completion Times

Schedule control charts were used for many years prior to the introduction of networks and naturally took some account of the interdependence of activities although the danger of overlooking a critical interrelationship in complex projects is obvious. The introduction of activity durations into a network enables analysis to be undertaken which leads to the scheduling of activities with an indication of spare time (float) associated with them.

A common convention is that the duration of each activity is contained below the half circle attached to each arrow. By working from left to right through the network, 'earliest event times' (the earliest times when events may occur) are determined and are shown in larger circles which are adjacent to the events which (unless they are perceived as milestones) are depicted by the small circles at the beginning and end of each arrow. The latest times when events may occur if the completion date is to be achieved (latest event times) are calculated by working backwards from the final event and are shown here in squares.

The computational procedure is simple and can be demonstrated by reference to a number of the activities included in Table 3.1. Assume that the student wishes to give consideration to the milestone which is achieved when his survey is completed (that is at the end of activity 13). If for simplicity activities 6 and 8 are ignored the network will include a total of 11 activites and one dummy (the broken arrow).

By taking account of activity durations it will be seen that the earliest time by which the survey will be completed is 34 weeks (remember that activity 2 cannot start until activity 4 has been completed). If 34 weeks is accepted by the student as the target towards which he will work the latest event times can be determined by subtraction. In Figure 3.2 the network is shown with a complete analysis of earliest and latest event times.

Whether or not an activity carries float is of great interest to the researcher. Several types of this may be recognised but it is sufficient for our purposes to consider 'total float'. This is the amount of spare time available to an activity if the starting event occurs as early as possible and the finishing event is allowed to take place as late as possible (that is without delaying the termination of the whole project). Several activities in Figure 3.2 possess total float:

Activity Number	Total Float (Weeks)
1	1
5	3
7	24
12	14

All of the remaining activities will be seen to have no total float and are said to be 'critical'. Information of this nature can be of the greatest help to students in scheduling their efforts. Of particular concern will be the path through the network which carries no total float (the 'critical path'). If any activities on the critical path take longer than planned the only way in

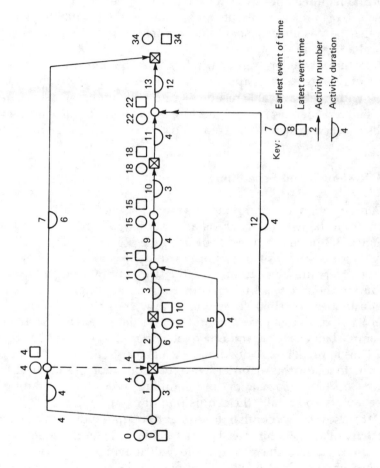

Figure 3.2   A network analysis to show earliest and latest event times

which the project will be completed on time will be a reduction in the duration of a subsequent activity on the critcal path.

It will be seen that 119 weeks is the estimate of the total time needed to complete the project network shown in Figure 3.1 provided there are no resource problems (see below). Given the time required for topic selection and the preparation of a research proposal this falls comfortably within the requirement of our hypothetical student's third objective of completing his project in about three years from his initial registration, given that he has already spent six months on preparing his research proposal and so on.

A feature of student research which is frequently alluded to is the scarcity of resources. Thus apparently parallel activities which would be feasible with freely available resources cannot be undertaken simultaneously. Full consideration must therefore be given to resource availability if realistic schedules are to be compiled.

7. Resources and Scheduling

In preparation for controlling the project a schedule may be derived directly from the network analysis as is shown in Figure 3.3.

Figure 3.3 permits a number of useful lessons to be drawn. Float is clearly indicated and provides an opportunity to smooth the demand for resources. Here the major resource is the student's time and although he will, during the first year, be committed to attempting to complete the critical activities on schedule he will if he wishes be able to plan non-critical activities so that peak demands on his time are reduced. It would for example be possible to undertake activities 5, 6, 7, 8 and 12 sequentially. Thus it might be decided first to select the participants for the pilot study and to follow this, in order, with the acquisition of statistical skills, decisions on target population and sampling procedures, drafting out three chapters and finally the acquisition of computing skills.

Of course it may occur that the demands on the student's time cannot be accommodated within the various activity floats available. Under those circumstances the project time will inevitably be extended. In assessing whether this is likely to happen it is important for the student not to overcommit himself. Experience shows that it is always a mistake to schedule 100 per cent of any resource on a project and this applies particularly to the student's own time during research. The project manager's usual rule of thumb would be to commit no more than 80 per cent of any resource leaving 20 per cent as a contingency margin. Obviously each individual student must assess the implications of this idea for the length of working day, which he will assume, in drawing up his research plan.

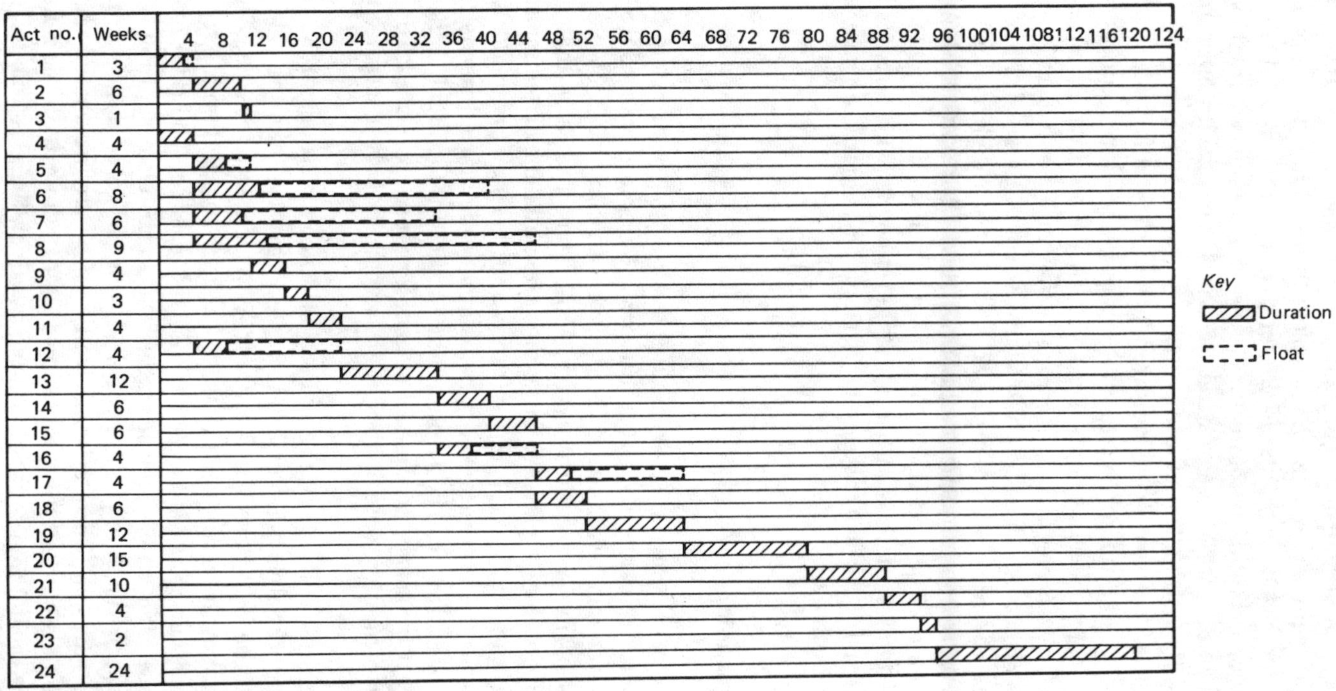

61

Figure 3.3   A schedule control chart based on the network analysis of figure 3.1

(Note that space is available to record the actual progress of each activity)

Over any length of time an average of 40 hours *effective* research work a week would seem adequate for most research projects particularly since this can be increased if progress is slower than desired. Excessively long hours of work should therefore be confined to times when they are unavoidable and should be restricted to a few weeks with appropriate periods of relaxation allowed afterwards.

The other resource considerations that may affect the project schedule relate to activities that are not under the student's control such as times at which lecture courses run or to constraints on access to hardware; for example, certain equipment may only be available during university vacations. Usually only a few such factors will affect any particular research project and can be adjusted for by intelligent use of the bar chart. Clearly these and other adjustments which involve the juggling of float are more easily coped with by making the bar chart 'adjustable' in some way. One method is to use a magnetic board, and another is to maintain the network on a computer so that new bar charts can be printed out almost instantaneously.

8. Replanning

It is evident that the seven points dealt with so far relate to the planning of the research. As soon as the project gets underway the role of the network changes from that of being purely a planning tool to one in which it is primarily a control device. Experience indicates that if the project is of any complexity two outcomes are inevitable. The first is that activity durations prove to be longer (rarely shorter) than planned and the second is that the ordering of activities still to be started needs to be amended. The former can be accommodated without too much difficulty; particularly if the basic schedule (that is before resources are taken into account) is computer generated. The latter can, however, create problems.

Because of the full-time student's need to complete his project by a specific date it is always necessary to have in front of him the extent of work yet to be completed. If the order in which activities need to be tackled changes (for example, access to data is delayed) then the student cannot be certain that his target date is still feasible. The only way to satisfy himself that this is so is to undertake a careful replanning which will involve a revision of the network. As this has to be done manually and as pressure may have arisen because of an unanticipated change foisted upon the student the temptation may exist to put off the redrawing. This can result in a situation arising in which there is little relationship between the network and the project work (this is often encountered outside the academic world). It is at these points that the student needs the self-discipline to spend some time on an activity (replanning) which does not immediately further his studies but which in the longer term may make the difference between completing on time and failing to do so.

RENDERING PROGRESS EXPLICIT : RESEARCH MILESTONES

There is space on the control chart to enter progress and the state of the study may be indicated by reference to a marker corresponding to the current week. This can be enhanced by filling in the duration allocated to each activity in a distinctive colour and marking the appropriate proportion of the bar below as work progresses in the same colour. This gives an immediate impression of which activities are ahead of schedule and which behind, provides a warning when dates begin to slip and, most importantly, provides a tangible measure of progress which can be very important in maintaining motivation as the project progresses.

A number of events in Figure 3.1 were designated milestones by the student. These are particularly important events during a project where progress can be reviewed and will normally be at the end of activities whose outcome is to some extent uncertain. As such they form a natural point at which to assess progress and determine whether the research plan is still feasible or whether it needs modification. Usually milestones will occur quite frequently but it is recommended that no more than three months should be allowed between them, since it is most undesirable that a longer period should pass without a major progress review.

The achievement of a milestone should be marked by just such a review involving at a minimum student and supervisor but quite possibly faculty members and students. This topic is discussed at greater length in Chapter 7.

THE ROLE OF NETWORK ANALYSIS DURING THE EXECUTION STAGE

The networks likely to be compiled by students will be much less complex than those used elsewhere and the task of redrawing should not therefore be too great. Nevertheless if they are to be employed throughout the research they should reflect with reasonable accuracy the view which the student has of the sequence of activities likely to be followed until the end of his work. In other words planning is not something that ceases once execution of the topic selected gets underway. Replanning may well need to carried out several times in the light of appraisals of previous progress.

THE ADVANTAGES OF NETWORK ANALYSIS

Some students may not be attracted towards the idea of using network analysis. Before rejecting the idea it is argued that consideration should be given to the following advantages:

a) The emphasis on rigorous planning, schedules and milestones is a notion to which students with limited time at their disposal should become accustomed.

b) If a network is used to plan a research study there is little likelihood that significant activities which need to be anticipated will be overlooked.

c) The levelling out of major peaks of demand on the researcher's time or the elimination of infeasible requirements for other resources may be possible.

d) In the event that planning indicates that despite the rough estimates included within the research proposal there would seem to be little prospect of achieving an acceptable completion date major or minor changes to plan may be made.

e) The efforts of the student will be focused on the achievement of the next milestone, thus providing a way of regularly reviewing progress as the project unfolds and identifying situations in which replanning is needed.

f) Motivation is generated by visual evidence of tasks completed, together with an awareness of the extent to which endeavour should be increased.

g) The network and the associated charts provide an excellent basis for communicating to others what activities remain to be completed and how they are linked, achievement to date and the schedule the researcher proposes to follow. The very fact that the supervisor is aware of progress is a considerable aid to keeping on schedule.

PLANNING PART-TIME RESEARCH

Most of the comments made so far in this chapter relate to full-time students. Part-time students have the added problem of planning their research so that it does not conflict with what is usually perceived as a full-time job. If the research is to be part of a mixed course involving study and project it is often assumed that the topic can be related to the nature of the student's full-time occupation. If this is not the case the student will need to give careful attention to the nature of the extra workload he is assuming.

Research for higher degrees in particular, with its need for extensive background reading, implies that this must be undertaken in the student's own time, even if data gathering may take place during his full-time employment. And of course in many instances the part-time student must confine the whole of his research to his nominal leisure time, realising that this will extend considerably the duration of his studies.

There is much to commend the use of network analysis by part-time students; the ordering of activities being as least as valuable an aid to planning as in the case of the full-time student. The major problem in constructing a control chart from an analysis based on activity durations is the sensible estimation of elapsed times. Although the work content will be similar to that involved in full-time studies the often unpredictable effect of the student's occupation (due to promotion, transfers, special projects and so on) will render estimates of time much more uncertain. Indeed it is worth pointing out that if research degree students encounter serious interruption to their plans they should consider requesting a suspension of their registration for a period which may be as long as two years. If the student is single-minded about his research though, and the nature of his job permits, then control through schedule charts compiled from network analysis is realistic. In other cases it may be more sensible to adopt an approach in which progress is simply marked up on the network. This will enable the part-time student to either take stock periodically or to consider the extent to which milestones are, or (more importantly) are not, being achieved.

If during the conduct of the research there is a total disaster in the sense that it becomes impossible (for example, if facilities for fieldwork are withdrawn) or pointless (for example, if it is discovered that the work has been done before, or if logical errors come to light) it becomes even more essential that the student is able to assess what may be achieved in the time left to him. The potential value of network analysis in these circumstances is obvious.

SUMMARY

PLANNING OF STUDENT RESEARCH: can demonstrate its feasibility within the time available by helping to identify all the activities which will be involved.

NETWORK ANALYSIS: although an additional task for the student, can be of great benefit in showing the interrelationships among activities and in providing the basis for a realistic control chart.

CONTROL CHARTS: enable the student to smooth out his efforts when a number of tasks may be addressed in parallel.

NETWORKS AND CONTROL CHARTS: which reflect progress can act as motivational devices as completed work is recorded.

PLANNING IS A CONTINUOUS PROCESS: and is much facilitated by the network analysis approach.

4

Literature Searching

INTRODUCTION

Most research work involves substantial use of published literature. Indeed the ability to ferret out obscure facts is often seen as the primary activity of the researcher and the regulations for research degrees always contain a requirement that the candidate should demonstrate the ability to make proper critical use of relevant literature. Accordingly the successful researcher needs to be able to do just this.

It is assumed that the reader is reasonably familiar with the use of libraries, particularly specialist and academic libraries. For our purpose the key features of such libraries are:

a) The existence of comprehensive catalogues. The catalogue of book stocks will be classified by author and class number, the latter in academic Anglo-Saxon libraries often being based on the Dewey system together with a classified subject index that allows the class number corresponding to a particular topic to be determined. In addition many libraries now catalogue books by title. Catalogues of periodical material will normally consist of lists of journals, and so on held and information on which issues are available.

b) Substantial collections of:

Primary sources – essentially the first publication of a piece of work;

Secondary sources – involving the indexing and classification of primary sources and the organisation of the information they contain into the general body of knowledge;

Tertiary sources – intended to facilitate the location of primary and secondary sources.

The sources that a researcher can use to carry out a literature search are listed in Table 4.1. Researchers should familiarise themselves with all the sources likely to be useful at the outset of their research. Academic libraries usually provide excellent tape/slide or film guides to their facilities and the way they are organised.

WHY SCAN THE LITERATURE?

There are two major reasons for carrying out a survey of the literature: a) as part of the process of topic selection, b) as part of the research project proper. Reference has been made in Chapter 2 to a variety of questions that need to be taken into account when selecting a topic. Thus there is the broad review of reported work in a field in the hope that previous authors will have suggested fruitful studies to be pursued by others. Equally, assessing the novelty of promising ideas will normally involve the researcher checking the literature to ensure that his proposed topic has not been tackled before and to define an area of study that he can consider his own.

Having selected his topic the researcher will normally need to carry out several surveys of relevant published literature(s) in rather greater depth. The preparation of a detailed research proposal will require the researcher to define previous work in his proposed fields and in those allied to it. Thus a study of the use of hovercraft in cross-Channel trans-

Primary sources

    Journal articles

    Conference proceedings

    Reports

    Government publications

    Patents

    Standards

    Catalogues, specifications, directories

Secondary sources

    Monographs

    Textbooks

    Review series (annals)

    Review papers in primary journals

    Journals covering specific literatures

    Subject abstracts

    Indexes of publications

    Current awareness / alerting services

Tertiary sources

    Handbooks

    Guides to specific literatures

    Subject bibliographies

    General bibliographies

    Encyclopedias

Table 4.1   Some literature sources

port would certainly not confine itself to that mode of transport alone. It would be necessary to examine other means of crossing the Channel so as to clarify the unique features of a hovercraft based service. Again it would probably be necessary to look at the use of hovercraft in ferry services elsewhere in the world to ascertain whether they are particularly well suited to cross-Channel operations. In assembling this wider picture the researcher would be able, when he presents his research findings, to make proper acknowledgement of the work of previous authors and to delineate his own contributions to the field.

As well as scanning the literatures of their chosen fields and related ones most researchers find it necessary to familiarise themselves with a rather different literature dealing with research tools appropriate to their topic. Thus geophysicists may well find it necessary to employ Fourier Transform methods in analysing and interpreting data signals. A social scientist on the other hand may need to attain a reasonable proficiency in the use of statistical methods. Most researchers accordingly have two broad types of literature search to do: the subject specific – closely related to the topic of interest – and that on research methodology. Usually the former will need to be pursued to considerably greater depth than the latter. It should be noted that some research projects involve the translation of methods devised in one field into another and normally require that an in-depth literature search to be carried out for both fields.

A number of different phases can be expected in the course of a literature search in accordance with the various stages of the research plan. Whatever the purpose of a particular phase, only limited resources are available for its execution. Almost always the restricted time that the researcher can devote to the task is the major constraint. Often there will be the additional problem that there are insufficient funds to borrow all the desired references from a central library such as the British Library Lending Division, or to pay for unlimited visits to a relevant specialist library. For this reason we shall examine various strategies for literature searching.

LITERATURE SEARCHES AND RELEVANCE TREES

A useful model of the literature searching process is to regard it as an exercise in the construction of a relevance tree of the type described in Chapter 2. At the topic level an initial keyword or subject, selected as a basis for searching, will lead to the discovery of further keywords derived from the early books and journals scanned. Some of these will lead to new literatures not directly related to that dealing with the initial subject. Each of these will in turn suggest further subject headings under which to search.

As an example of a relevance tree Figure 4.1 shows one set of subjects that might be scanned in defining a topic within the broad framework 'Interviewing in social work'. The figure shows how starting from the subject 'Interviewing in social work' three broad subject areas have been selected namely: 'Interviewing in general', the 'Role of interviewing in social work theory', and the 'Role of interviewing in social work practice'. These have in turn been used to suggest further subjects. Though at this stage it is not necessary to pursue any of the subjects in depth it will be assumed that having advanced the search as shown in Figure 4.1 the researcher has gained sufficient feel for the literature of each to decide that the research will focus on the 'Effectiveness of the casework interview' and that important related subjects will be 'Interview techniques and counselling interviews'. At a later stage each of these subjects will probably form the starting point for another phase of the literature search. This example is, however, typical in that it involves:

– the generation of a number of alternative subjects/key words;
– deciding which subjects to pursue;
– deciding which subjects to abandon;
– deciding when sufficient effort has been put in for the purpose in hand so that the process can be (temporarily) halted.

To carry out these four activities effectively we need ways of generating new subjects – since without a touch of inventiveness at the start our search is likely to be fairly superficial. Conversely without criteria for abandoning lines of enquiry the literature search rapidly gets out of hand.

The Generation of Alternative Subjects

Once the literature search is successfully underway, finding new, related, subjects ceases to be a problem. In practice the difficulty of getting started can vary enormously from one subject to another, thus the researcher who has only a few weeks available to conduct his work should stick to the rule that if he cannot get his literature search beyond the stage of looking for new subject areas within a couple of hours, he should select another topic. He can, therefore, restrict his efforts to looking at three sources of ideas:

i) the alphabetical subject index;

    ii) encyclopedias/guides and handbooks;
    iii) thesauri/dictionaries

The alphabetical subject index provides a quick and convenient way of finding related subject areas or alternative terms for the same keyword. It also provides a rough and ready guide to the volume of literature in a particular area, since, broadly speaking, a subject area is extensively subdivided only if a substantial amount has been written on it. Once a subject has been identified the subject index will provide its class number. The classified catalogue can then be consulted to provide a list of all books that belong to that particular classification. A useful trick is therefore to find one relevant book, ascertain its subject classification and then consult the classified catalogue for other similar books.

Usually journals cover a much wider range of subjects and therefore cannot be classified as precisely as books. Nevertheless some classification scheme should exist for them that will enable the student to locate journals most likely to be relevant. In many fields the PERMUTERM *Subject Indexes of the Social Science Citation Index*, the *Science Citation Index* and the *Arts and Humanities Citation Index* to be discussed later provide an alternative way of constructing the relevance tree.

Encyclopedias provide an excellent method of getting a quick feel for a subject and a picture of knowledge in that field and related areas. It should be remembered that as well as general encyclopedias such as the *Encyclopedia Britannica* a variety of more specialist guides and handbooks exist on particular subjects (cf. Walford, 1975).

Where a topic cannot be found in an encyclopedia or guide, dictionaries are useful for suggesting terms having a similar meaning which can be looked up instead. Note that some fields, for example, social science, have their own dictionaries. A further possibility is to use a thesaurus, that is a list of alternative terms for the same concept. As well as general thesauri such as *Roget's Thesaurus* certain specialist libraries maintain ones specific to the field they cover. The researcher with more time to spare can often profitably make use of additional sources of ideas as discussed later.

Deciding which Subjects to Abandon

Given our broad interest in effective management of student research a word of caution is appropriate at this point. Though many research projects may involve fields that are developing rapidly (for example, microcomputers in the late 1970s) the researcher must limit the time he spends scanning the literature if he is not to prejudice other activities.

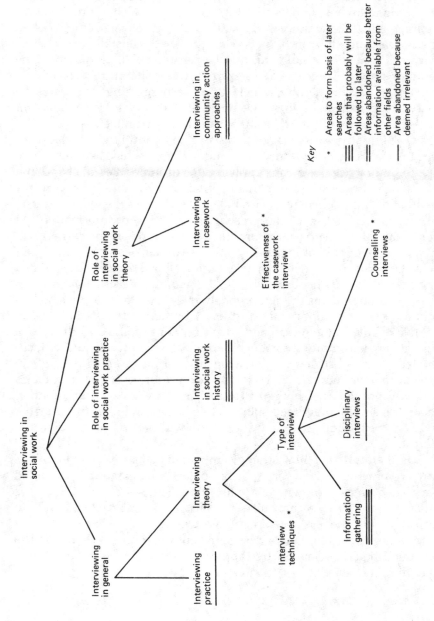

Key

*   Areas to form basis of later searches
≡   Areas that probably will be followed up later
=   Areas abandoned because better information available from other fields
—   Area abandoned because deemed irrelevant

Interviewing in social work

Interviewing in general

Role of interviewing in social work practice

Role of interviewing in social work theory

Interviewing in community action approaches

Interviewing in casework

Effectiveness of * the casework interview

Interviewing practice

Interviewing theory

Interviewing in social work history

Interview techniques *

Type of interview

Information gathering

Disciplinary interviews

Counselling * interviews

Figure 4.1   A subject relevance tree for the first stages of a literature search

Without mechanisms for deciding which lines of enquiry not to pursue most literature searches soon get completely out of control. For this reason many researchers adopt the often somewhat arbitrary rule of scanning only 'the literature of the subject'. In some well-defined fields, for example, nuclear science, such a strategy is very sensible. In other less clear areas such as economics this may be detrimental to the quality of the literature survey. Thus as well as examining the literature of industrial relations the researcher in the field of wage bargaining might well be advised to consider the literature of conflict theory which would not necessarily be considered relevant to the industrial relations specialist.

If the literature search is not to be confined within the straitjacket of 'the literature' other ways must be found to decide which avenues not to explore. In practice this means applying one of three rules: a) abandon it because it is irrelevant to the area of interest; b) ignore it because the literature of some other subject (to be) studied covers the ideas better; c) do not pursue further for the present since sufficient information has been obtained for the purpose for which the search is being carried out. Thus in the example of Figure 4.1 our researcher has not further sub-divided the asterisked items because though all will need to be examined further enough work has been done on them for the present. Similarly the triply underlined items though probably relevant in a later phase of the literature search do not require further elaboration at this stage. As an example of rule b) the researcher's decision not to follow up the role of interviewing in community action based social work (doubly underlined) is noted. This is because interviewing plays a far more central role in casework and as such it is unlikely that the literature of community based work will provide insights not available from the casework literature. Finally the singly underlined subjects have been excluded from further study on the grounds that they are probably irrelevant to the subject of interest.

The literature searching strategy embodied in Figure 4.1 whereby the search commences with a very specific subject and is gradually extended into related areas is of general applicability. The search should always start with the most specific subject definition the researcher is able to supply. Where there is a copious literature he may never need to go beyond this initial subject to amass sufficient references. Where less has been published the relevance tree approach provides a systematic way of expanding the search.

CITATION RELEVANCE TREES

Most articles of a research nature cite previous work, and in doing so tend to reference seminal books and articles in the field of interest. Major articles in that field not only provide a useful way into past literature but also with the help of the citation indexes, into journal articles published at a later date. The principle of the *Science Citation Index* and the *Social Science Citation Index* is a simple one. For each article by a particular author, the *Citation Index* lists articles that have cited it in a particular interval. This provides a way of picking up subsequent articles on the same subject. Reference to the index then provides a list of papers cited by those authors. Figure 4.2 shows an example of a forward literature search using the *Science Citation Index*. The general field of interest of the researcher is the topic of computer security. From an article by Weiss, published in 1974 it is possible to construct a relevance tree extending forward in time. The citation indexes provide an effective way of carrying out a literature search in many fields. Because they deal with fairly recent journal articles (plus certain books) they are most useful for subjects that are evolving rapidly. In such fields most publications of relevance to the researcher are likely to be found in journal articles published in the past few years. Conversely in fields such as history where articles published several decades ago may well be extremely relevant or in fields where most important reference material is to be found in books, the citation indexes are less useful. Nevertheless in many fields they provide at a very minimum an important check that no major articles have been overlooked and the reader who is unfamiliar with them is advised to consult the citation indexes themselves for further information on their use.

Closing Off the Citation Tree

Just as it is necessary to restrict the growth of a subject relevance tree so too the researcher needs to find ways of halting the growth of the citation tree. Two ideas are particularly useful here. Firstly, the notion of core references. In any reasonably established field certain books embody the key ideas of the subject and this is evidenced by the frequency with which they are cited by other authors. Similarly any particular field of research will have core journals in which any major work in the area is most likely to be published. Defining core books and journals restricts the citation tree by limiting the citations that will be followed up to those publications. Armed with the names of core journals the researcher can rapidly extend his list by using the volume to identify those journals that carry most of the references cited by authors of papers in the journals already known to him.

The notion of core journals is used by librarians in many subject areas as a basis for bibliographic services such as lists of current contents of journals or for deciding which journal articles should be abstracted. Accordingly, examination of the journals scanned in preparing bibliographic information provides one quick way of establishing the core journals. An alternative method that can sometimes be used is to examine the volume of the *Science* (*Social Science* or *Arts and Humanities*) *Citation Index* that provides information on the frequency with which articles in a specified journal cite other journals.

The scope of a search may be reduced by setting a publication date prior to which references will not be followed up. Obviously the date set must depend on the field. A guide is easily obtained in libraries that date stamp books on issue. The concept of the half life of journals is well established and finds practical embodiment in many large academic libraries in that only the latest years of a journal are readily accessible. For years which precede the half life other modes of storage are often adopted – for example restricted access stacks. Obviously the cut-off date varies from subject to subject. In rapidly changing fields like particle physics it may be only a few years ago whereas in fields such as economics or social history, publications dating back fifty years or more may well be very useful.

It should be remembered that for a preliminary search in a field the cut-off date need not be set very far back since most authors refer to and summarise the work of their predecessors. The literature of the past ten or twenty years will therefore usually provide a reasonable outline of the field for fifty years or more. If at a later stage of searching it appears that significant work on the subject was published before the cut-off date it must obviously be positioned earlier. As a concrete instance of this twofold approach we may take the notion of 'continental drift' that was important to the development of the theory of plate tectonics. The student of geomorphology in the early 1960s would have had little difficulty in finding references to the continental drift hypothesis put forward by Wegener, fifty years before, Though summaries of the idea were often sceptical and frequently dismissive, they nonetheless provided a sufficient basis for understanding the key concepts. Thus a student carrying out a preliminary search in this field needed only to examine books and articles published say up to fifteen years previously. If eventually, he decided that it was relevant to his research topic then he could have gone back to the work of Wegener and, indeed, earlier workers. In effect his cut-off date would probably have needed to be moved back to 1900.

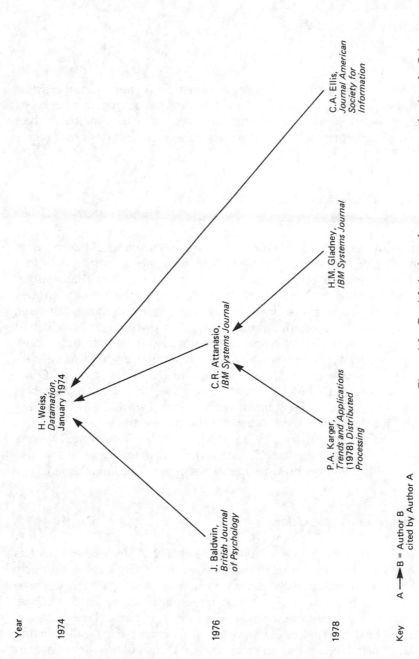

Year

1974   H. Weiss,
        Datamation,
        January 1974

1976   C.R. Attanasio,
        IBM Systems Journal

1978   P.A. Karger,
        Trends and Applications
        (1978) *Distributed*
        Processing

        H.M. Gladney,
        IBM Systems Journal

        C.A. Ellis,
        Journal American
        Society for
        Information

        J. Baldwin,
        British Journal
        of Psychology

Key   A ——▶ B = Author B
              cited by Author A

*Figure 4.2   Partial citation relevance tree constructed using the Science
Citation Index*

SOME USEFUL SOURCES

Most searches are likely to rely mainly on books and journal articles. Since these are familiar items they need no further comment. Other types of source are, however, used much more frequently in some fields than others and therefore their special advantages warrant further consideration.

Reports/Occasional Papers

In many fields technical reports can be a major source of information. It may well be, therefore, that the more complete account given in a technical report will be of greater use to the researcher than journal articles on the subject. Furthermore the reports of certain research groups are sufficiently prestigious for the researchers concerned to favour them as a method of disseminating their results. The upshot is that as well as being more comprehensive research reports are often more up to date. Similar remarks apply to the occasional papers which tend to be published by many research units particularly in the social sciences. Obviously this is a special category of material and details of it are usually best obtained through special guides such as the *British Library Lending Division (BLLD) Announcement Bulletin* in the UK and through the *Scientific Technical and Aerospace Reports (STAR)* index and the Government *Reports Announcements and Index (GRAI)* in the US. In many cases these also provide information on how a copy of the report can be obtained.

Theses and Dissertations

At the doctoral level it is necessary to establish that the researcher has made an original contribution to knowledge. Accordingly it will normally be necessary to check that no theses on the lines the researcher proposes have been published. Major academic libraries carry lists of these accepted for higher degrees in various countries, in particular Britain and the USA. The BLLD *Announcement Bulletin,* for example, as well as listing reports, translations and so on produced by British Government organisations, industry and academic institutions also lists most doctoral theses produced at British universities. The *ASLIB Index to theses accepted for higher degrees by the universities of Great Britain and Ireland and the Council of*

National Academic Awards covers theses produced as a result of a research study plus certain others. Since the *ASLIB Index* tends to be one or two years behind it is useful to be able to supplement this by information from *Research in British Universities, Polytechnics and Colleges,* which covers most types of research work. From the appropriate volume of this publication the researcher can identify and contact the workers in UK academic institutions most likely to be carrying out and supervising research in his area.

For theses published in the USA similar information can be obtained from *Dissertation Abstracts*.

Government Publications

The amount of material published on behalf of governments is enormous and forms an important reference source for many types of research. Indeed, for much UK research they are a major secondary data source. For this reason they will be considered in more detail in Chapter 6.

Because of the sheer volume of material produced most academic libraries classify government publications separately, very often outside the normal subject index system. Accordingly, the researcher needs to ascertain whether important material is to be found under government publications and, if so, find how to obtain it in the libraries he uses. In the UK, for instance, this will mean consulting the annual, monthly or daily lists of material published by HMSO or the *Catalogue of British Official Publications not published by HMSO*. In the US monthly lists of the US Government Publications Office provide similar information.

Standards/Codes of Practice

Standards can be an important source of information in technological fields since the introduction of new standards may well spawn considerable development activity and in some markets is a major determinant of product performance. For the latter reason standards, and the similar codes of practice, may also be important as a data source for the researcher interested in the history of some aspect of technology. In the UK the most important source of standards is the British Standards Institution, with similar roles in the US being fulfilled by the American National Standards Institute, and in Germany by DIN standards.

Outside science and engineering most professional bodies also publish standards or codes of practice with which their members are expected to comply. In the accounting field in the UK, for example, the Institute of Chartered Accountants plays a major role in determining accounting standards.

Patents

In many types of applied research in technology patents are important either because they indicate new techniques and methods to solve particular problems or because they suggest further inventions that did not occur to the originator of the patent. They also provide an important data source for researchers interested in the history or economics of invention and innovation.

Information on patents appears in a number of indexing and abstracting services. Copies of British patents are available in the UK from what are essentially regional patent deposit libraries. Ideas are usually patented in more than one country, so using a concordance of patents which gives the number assigned to the application for the same patent in different countries makes it possible to find, say, the British application corresponding to a patent that was first taken out in Japan.

Trade Journals and Newspapers

In certain types of research trade journals and newspapers can be important data sources. This is particularly true of the former which often carry information that is not recorded elsewhere.

Practice with regard to the storage of trade journals varies widely in the UK. Few libraries, save the Copyright Libraries[1] take more than a small fraction of those published reflecting the fact that many of them are most unlikely to be used again once they cease to be current. Furthermore many of those that are taken are not bound, with the result that individual issues may disappear. For these reasons such material is often not all that easy to use and the researcher may well find it worthwhile going to a specialist library for it.

The position is somewhat better as far as UK national newspapers are concerned as there are a number of commercial indexing services available for the quality press at least. The *Research Index*, for example, provides listings of all mentions of larger companies and industries in major

1. The libraries entitled under UK law to a copy of every book published in the UK, namely the British Library, the libraries of Oxford and Cambridge Universities, the Library of Trinity College, Dublin, the National Library of Scotland and, for some books, the National Library of Wales Aberystwyth.

newspapers. *The Times Index* provides an index to materials contained in the various newpapers of the Times Group itself. Nowadays microfilm or microfiche copies of major newspapers are available which though somewhat inconvenient to use do ensure that copies of fairly recent material are available.

Where local newspapers are concerned matters are more complex. It is unlikely that any formal index is available and therefore it may be necessary to work through them systematically for the period of interest if that was some time ago. For relatively current material, however, excellent advice may well be available from the newspaper's own libraries.

Ephemera

Much material is not stored in the library in the usual way and, indeed, may not be catalogued. Examples are company reports, trade literature such as specifications of products, catalogues, price lists, opera programmes, notices of forthcoming sales, applications for planning consents, and so on. Such items are not published in the formal sense and are generally referred to by librarians as ephemera because they are useful only for a brief period.

Libraries generally, however, have no obligation to stock ephemera and individual items are likely to be traceable only if they are of sufficient interest to collectors for a catalogue to have been published, for example, Victorian Christmas cards, or they form part of a recognised collection of historical material that has been properly catalogued. The only useful counsel that can be offered to all but the very experienced researcher is that if circumstances warrant an attempt should be made to solicit the support of an expert on ephemera in the field of interest.

Abstracts

In many fields one or more abstracting services exist that give resumés of the contents of journal articles and/or patents. Such services are usually reasonably up to date (up to one year behind) and will normally cover a wider range of journals in the field than are available in all except the very largest libraries. They are accordingly of great utility to the researcher who finds a reference to an article in a journal not kept by his own library. Under those circumstances it will normally be necessary in the UK to order a copy from the BLLD, a process that costs several pounds (when all costs are taken into account) and which will also usually take over a week. Obviously there is virtue in studying an abstract, to find out whether the article is likely to be worth reading or merely duplicates material already studied.

Most abstracting services classify articles in accordance with the subjects they cover; they also provide an indexing service. Services of this type therefore provide an alternative approach to carrying out a literature search aimed at finding articles on a particular topic.

CARRYING OUT A LITERATURE SEARCH

Figure 4.3 includes a number of flowcharts that summarise the major features of literature searching. The variety of subjects and the numerous possible purposes of a literature search inevitably mean that the reader will need to adapt the advice given to his particular circumstances. To aid that process each of the charts will now be discussed in order and the major assumptions they involve will be outlined:

(a) Overall Flowchart for a Literature Search (Chart 1).

This gives a broad picture of the process of carrying out a literature search. Often the researcher will have access to relevant theses or dissertations in which case he should begin with these. Also he may know a number of references (possibly by author's name) in the field. Where references are known the researcher may wish to be sure that these are comprehensive prior for example, to putting together the final version of a thesis (this is a special need and is dealt with in Chart 4). If this is not his aim and he knows of some key papers, his knowledge of the field is almost certainly sufficient to base his literature search on journal articles (Chart 3).

If none of the above apply, then the researcher is more or less starting from scratch. In that case the alphabetical subject index is usually the best place to begin. This gives the class number of each subject. Once the relevant class number is obtained, the classified subject catalogue should then be consulted to find the names of all books on the subject held by the library.

If the search is initially to be based on books the researcher may well hope to find bibliographies which list relevant books and indeed journals. Having exhausted these sources of references it may then be appropriate to turn to government publications. At this point if the library concerned does not list all its own theses and dissertations in the classified subject catalogue a check should be made using the various abstracts of theses and dissertations to locate any relevant ones available in the researcher's own library. Alternatively he can request theses and dissertations from other universities, provided he is willing to wait the necessary length of time for them to be obtained. (The time needed to obtain a thesis, particularly one presented at a foreign institution, can vary markedly depending on the subject and the institution. It is, therefore, worthwhile getting an estimate of the time needed from a librarian). Finally if the researcher wishes he may broaden the area of search and return to an earlier point in the flowchart.

In general the search will terminate when either the new references being generated are to material already examined or to unimportant sources or where the researcher has reached the limit of the time or money he is willing to devote to the particular search. In many fields the complete execution of all the stages shown on this chart would involve impossible amounts of effort and much pointless reduplication of references. In recognition of this fact, we have indicated on this chart and subsequent ones, convenient breakpoints or milestones where the researcher may take stock and decide whether he has gone far enough for his purpose.

It should be remembered that in the longer research project, at least, there will usually be several stages of literature searching. Hardly ever will the student need to find all references on his chosen subject. Rather he must continually ask himself, 'Is this relevant to my research? For what chapter is this material needed? Will this article provide sufficient new material to be useful?'

(b) Following up a Book (Chart 2)

The major assumption of this chart is that it is much easier to obtain books that are in the catalogue of a library to which one has ready access than to obtain them via inter-library loans or visits to specialist libraries. Indeed the two latter sources are increasingly subject to budgetary restrictions. Where some older books are concerned it may be difficult to provide full bibliographic details, that is, title, publisher, and so on. Under these circumstances it will be necessary to consult suitable catalogues such as the British Museum General Catalogue of Printed Books or the US Library of Congress National Union Catalog so that the researcher can be confident that the book will arrive if ordered.

84

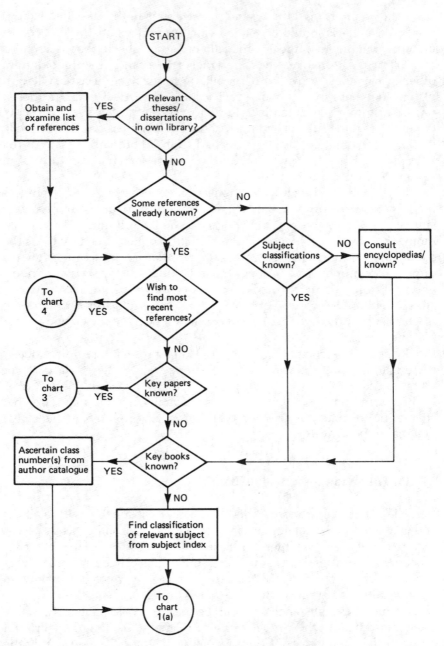

Figure 4.3   Flowcharts summarising literature search processes

Chart 1   Overall flowchart for literature search

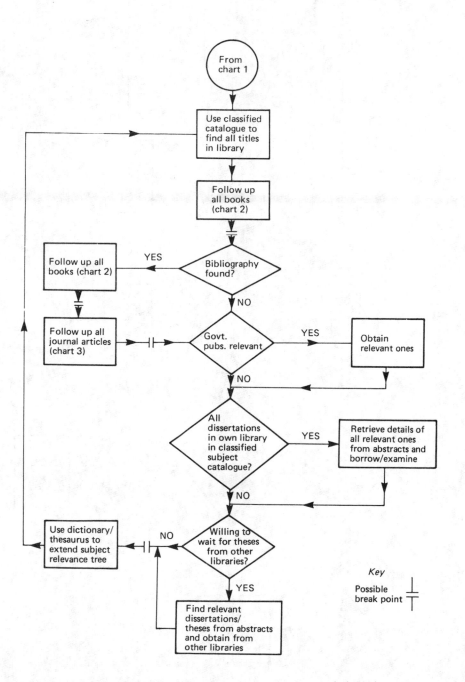

Chart 1(a)   Overall flowchart for literature search (cont.)

86

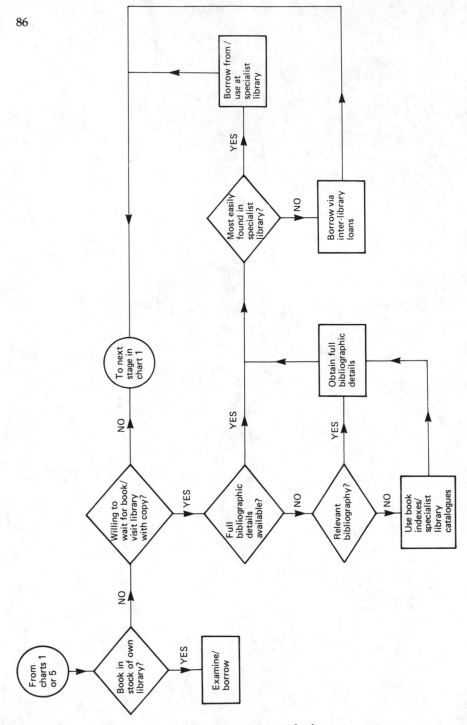

Chart 2 Following up a book

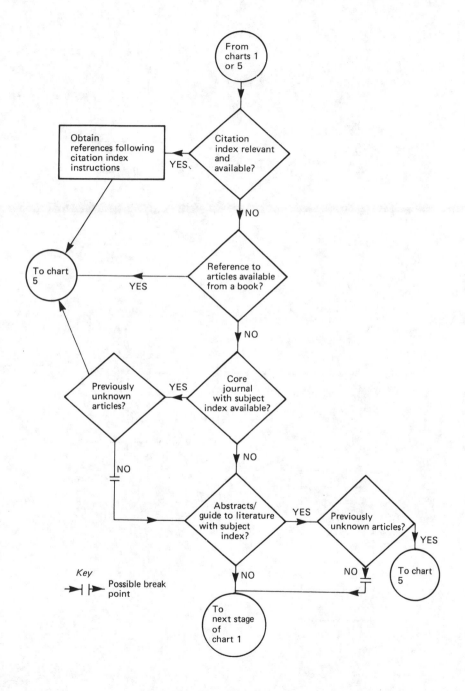

Chart 3   Finding Articles

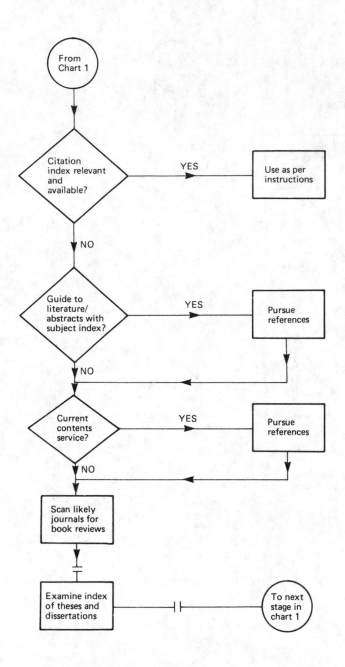

Chart 4   Finding Recent References

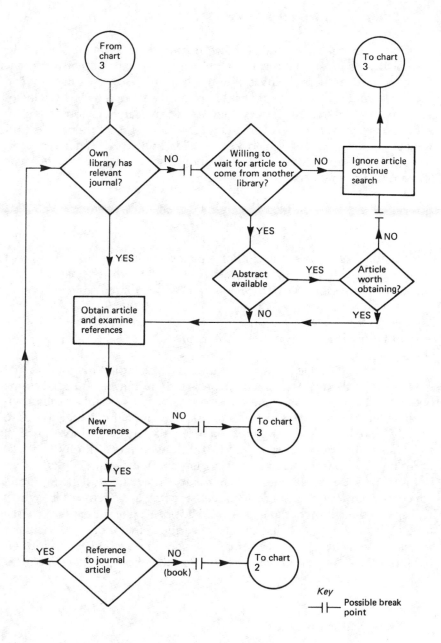

Chart 5   Following up an article

(c) **Finding Articles (Chart 3)**

This chart deals with the broad principles of obtaining references to journal articles given that certain references to them are already known. The conditions under which citation indexes are likely to be useful have already been discussed. Where these are fulfilled and they are available, they are a natural starting place. Otherwise the researcher should identify either a core journal or a set of abstracts with a subject index and find subject headings under which key articles known to him have been classified. These same subject classifications can then be used as the basis for retrieving other articles.

(d) **Finding Recent References (Chart 4)**

Again, if applicable, the citation indexes are usually the best way of ensuring that a literature search is up to date. Alternatively, abstracting or current awareness services if available can be used for the same purpose.

(e) **Following up an Article (Chart 5)**

As with books, it is far easier to make use of an article in a journal that is stocked by the researcher's own library than it is to wait for it to be obtained from elsewhere. Where the journal is not stocked all the previously noted budgetary restrictions are likely to apply but, since there are usually more articles than books on a topic, perhaps with more force. It follows that the researcher needs to think even more carefully before ordering articles from other libraries than about ordering books.

Whereas the researcher's own library may not stock the journal concerned it may well subscribe to an abstracting or review service which will enable the researcher to gain a good impression of the contents of the article. Usually the article itself will cite various other works, particularly if it is a review article. These, of course should be followed up in their turn, provided the researcher is happy that the effort involved is worthwhile.

Using a Citation Index

The principle of a citation index has already been outlined. While there are few subjects for which a literature search can be conducted solely using a citation index, there are many topics for which the use of the *Science Citation Index, Social Science Citation Index* or the *Arts and Humanities Citation Index* forms a natural starting point. The major knowledge they assume is the names of one or two important authors in the field or some familiarity with the technical terms used in the broad area of study, and a general knowledge of how to use the academic literature. In particular they have the advantage that they are usually to be found on a single shelf within the library, often close to abstracts and other bibliographical material. The researcher can then more quickly build up a bibliography of references than if he were to derive them from individual articles in different journals, which might well be in different physical locations and certainly will not follow a consistent set of standards with regard to indexes and so on. Also searches start from the name of a relevant author and this fits the way in which researchers mentally file details of major papers in their field. However, the citation indexes do not work equally well in all subjects. Fields where articles make relatively little use of citation or where references are to personal communications pose problems as do references to works whose relationship to the research being described is tenuous or which have been superseded by better ones. The researcher must expect therefore that their use will lead to a certain proportion of unfruitful references and he must decide whether these are likely to be adequately compensated for by the successful ones.

COMPUTER SEARCHES

There are now many bibliographic databases that can be accessed by the researcher using an on-line computer terminal. A notable example is the Lockheed Dialog System which, at the time of writing comprises some seventy databases on different subjects. Comprehensive lists of such databases can be found in: the EUSIDIC Database Guide (Tomberg, 1978).

A bibliographic database contains a list of articles, patents, reports and so on covering specific fields. Usually only the titles of the articles are recorded on the database, though sometimes additional keywords may be appended to give a better description of the article's contents. The detailed way in which a search is conducted varies from one database to another. The general principle, however, is that various descriptors are provided by the user and all articles whose titles or associated keywords match these descriptors are printed out by the system. Thus the descriptor:

SEWER *and* (MAINTENANCE *or* REPAIR)

will result in all articles whose titles (or keywords) contain the words SEWER(S) and MAINTENANCE in either order, or the words SEWER(S) and REPAIR in either order being printed out.

Such databases have three disadvantages: they require a trained librarian or experienced user to access the system; they contain only relatively recent articles extending back perhaps fifteen years, and their use has to be paid for (the cost of a typical search being perhaps £40 in the UK). Because cost depends on the number of references it is important either to begin the search with a very specific referencing term as described earlier or to request details only of references that cover similar subjects to a key reference supplied by the user.

Databases are designed for international use (The Lockheed system is in California) and therefore can spread the very large cost of maintaining them over a worldwide clientele. In many cases they are capable of generating a wider set of reference material on many topics than would be possible by conventional means. It is likely therefore that their importance to researchers will grow considerably as the amount of information held on them increases. The research student contemplating a research career may well find it worth mastering their use – should funds permit!

SETTING UP ONE'S OWN BIBLIOGRAPHY

The computer databases embody a principle that is important for the individual researcher – the results of a literature search need to be incorporated in the researcher's own bibliography. Sooner or later some or all of his references will have to be compiled into a list for a thesis or an article in an academic journal. They must, therefore, be recorded in sufficient detail to facilitate this process and preferably in such a way that the multiplicity of different referencing standards, for example, numbered in order of appearance, listed in alphabetical order, are readily accommodated. Furthermore a good bibliography in any new field is a very tradeable commodity and the researcher who possesses one is likely to find that if he makes it available to other researchers they will in turn make their data available to him. Certainly for students who come after him (including perhaps his own research students) such a bibliography is invaluable.

For these reasons we shall now discuss how the research student can set up his own computer bibliography. As computer terminals and microcomputers become widely available the effort involved in developing such a database is little different from that required to record the necessary information manually particularly since many researchers and librarians have already written software for this purpose. If the researcher is disinclined to use the computer a variety of proprietary systems – mainly based on punched cards – are available that can be used to implement the ideas outlined below.

A bibliographic database can only be set up if certain standards are adopted. It should be remembered that a system intended for use mainly by one or few researchers need not have the sophistication of a commercial system; the user needs only to adopt a set of conventions that suit him. This will usually involve carrying the following information for each reference:

1. *Author(s)/editor(s)*
    Type of work; book, paper, thesis, for instance
    and for example

for a book	*for a journal article*
title	title of paper
edition	name of journal
number of volumes	volume
publisher	issue
place of publication	page numbers
date of publication	year

2. A set of KEYWORDS describing the contents of the work
3. Supplementary information

Given that a comprehensive set of details are recorded the biggest problems likely to be encountered are: a) spelling errors which can easily be removed if each reference is checked after entry; b) the transliteratign of certain foreign names, where different publishers and writers adopt different conventions, for instance Dostoevsky, Dostoevski. The remedy for the latter problem is for the researcher to adopt one standard and stick to it. Provided he is consistent all occurrences of this name can be edited to some other form at a later date, if desired.

It is suggested that in Section 2 of the reference, keywords are given describing the work in question. The individual researcher should give them serious consideration, since their use makes possible much more effective searches within the database. Given the restricted amount of information that can be incorporated in a title (particularly in the case of books), and the fact that titles can mislead as to contents, if searches are based on title alone a number of relevant references will be missed.

To implement a keyword system the researcher needs to set up his own thesaurus of keywords for indexing purposes. This must be sufficiently detailed for a precise description of the contents of any work to be given but should remain reasonably small. It should be remembered that there will often be synonymous terms. In such cases one should be chosen as the thesaurus term and a note should be made under the synonyms of the term actually adopted. In general for one researcher a thesaurus of a few hundred terms should suffice. Nevertheless maintenance of the thesaurus is made easier by keeping that on the computer also.

The use of keywords means that the researcher needs to provide a list for each of the references he reads. This is a useful discipline and is a way of making at least brief notes on a reference and is a check on whether the researcher has understood it. Nor need the number of terms used be particularly large; the aim, after all, is to categorise the article or book not reproduce it. In fact, in practice, a dozen or so terms seems quite adequate in most fields for all save the exceptional work.

The third section of the record allowing supplementary information to be recorded is usually also worthwhile. It normally causes little trouble to design such a feature into the system from the outset even if, initially, it is not used. To incorporate it later, however, may well be more difficult. This type of facility is useful because most researchers need to record additional information about some references, for example, which libraries hold it, or the researcher's opinion of the work.

SERENDIPITY IN LITERATURE SEARCHING

The preceding sections have been concerned with the execution of a formal literature search. While at this point the importance of mastering the procedures involved, is re-emphasised, it is worth reminding the student that there are also benefits to be gained from relatively unplanned, intermittent and informal searching activities. Browsing in sections of the library where books related to the field of study are stocked provides one such method. Regular inspection of the new titles shelf to be found in most libraries provides another. Casual observation of the books and journals other researchers – perhaps in very different fields – are using is a third way. A lively curiosity about, and a good general knowledge of, one's field of study are also very useful and these can be promoted by regular reading of book reviews in the quality press and in specialist journals.

In the short term it is unlikely that such activities will lead to any benefit in conducting a specific literature research. Most researchers would agree, however, that in the long term they do substantially enhance the quality of their literature searches, and reduce the time required to carry them out.

THE ROLES OF THE SUPERVISOR AND THE LIBRARIAN

In practice, of course, the help the student receives from both his supervisor and from specialist librarians may well be greater than that he gets from pursuing the formal literature search discussed above. This is particularly true in the shorter research project or the early days of research. Usually a supervisor will know the key references in a field and the main people working in it, so that the research student is saved much preliminary spadework. Similarly the subject specialist librarian can be relied on for information about core references and core journals as well as information about pertinent abstracting services. Nonetheless being able to use the literature effectively is an important part of the researcher's craft. The research student should therefore demonstrate that he has mastered it to the extent that he can pay his way by helping newcomers to his subject to carry out literature searches and by finding references that are useful to his colleagues and his supervisor. If he can do this he need feel no qualms in turn in asking for assistance in those cases where he genuinely needs it.

USING THE REFERENCES

Finally, it should be remembered that successful identification of relevant references is only part of the story. Unless the information they contain can be purposefully used as detailed in the next chapters the researcher is left with little more than an impressive bibliography, which may well prove counterproductive if he cannot demonstrate the ability to use it well. It may well be therefore that the study of a book such as Leedy (1956) on reading skills – including the improvement of comprehension as well as reading speed – may prove a worthwhile investment.

SUMMARY

> LITERATURE SEARCHES ARE NECESSARY: for topic selection and as part of the research proper.

> SUBJECT AND CITATION RELEVANCE TREES: are effective strategies to adopt in literature searching.

> USEFUL SOURCES ARE: abstracts, theses, dissertations, research reports, government publications, pamphlets, newspapers and ephemera.

> LITERATURE SEARCH FLOWCHARTS: suggest that a systematic approach to the process can be adopted.

> BIBLIOGRAPHIC COMPUTER SEARCHES: though quite expensive at present are likely to be an increasingly used research technique.

> INDIVIDUAL BIBLIOGRAPHIES: set up and maintained by the research student are much to be commended.

PART B:

DATA ANALYSIS
AND GATHERING

5

Analysing the Data

THE ROLE OF ANALYSIS

As pointed out in Chapter 2 until a feasible outline of the type of analysis to be undertaken has been determined the research plan must be considered incomplete. Many students are tempted to embark on literature searches and massive programmes of data gathering before thinking about how the results are to be analysed. All too often this leads to considerable wasted effort. Essential items of data are not collected, or the first attempts at analysis are too trivial so that a complete rethink is necessary.

One key function of analysis is to communicate the value (whether academic, social or scientific) of the findings. An even more important purpose is to convince the reader that through the innate value of the knowledge gained the research report makes a sufficient contribution for the level of research in question and that the research measures up to the necessary standards of academic worth. For this reason at the doctoral level there is a flavour of the legal process about analysis. It should be seen that it was done for good cause and that it was properly carried out. At the lower levels of a research project, of course, such exalted standards may not come into play. Rather, given the crucial role of analysis in the research process, the primary aim of requiring the student to carry out a research project may well be to enable him to develop the ability to evaluate the analysis of other researchers. Such requirements are usually evident, for example, in university regulations for dissertations produced as part of a master's degree, with their emphasis on 'an ordered presentation of knowledge in a particular field' or 'a critical exposition of previous work'.

DEFINITION OF ANALYSIS

For the purposes of this chapter analysis will be assumed to involve the ordering and structuring of data to produce knowledge. Data will be interpreted broadly as information gathered by observation, through books or pictures, field surveys, laboratory experiments, etc. The chapter will cover approaches to analysis that can be applied in a variety of different fields. As such it addresses two topics often separated in texts on research methodology, namely research design and data analysis. In practice these are closely interlinked – at least in principle – since the design determines the data and what can be done with it, whereas the end purposes of the data analysis are the major determinants of the research design. For this reason we deal here with both aspects.

The definition of analysis proposed is a broad one and it will be presumed to embrace a whole range of activities of both the qualitative and the quantitative type. Nevertheless there is a discernible tendency for all research to make increasing use of quantitative analysis and in particular statistical methods. The latter enjoy a special position in research because they grew up through attempts by mathematicians to provide solutions to problems of scientific investigations noted by philosophers. Furthermore they reflect the structure of the analysis process in many different fields. Inevitably, then, the bias of this chapter is towards statistical methods. Even so there are still a large number of other such methods. Rather than give a detailed account of some techniques, which would inevitably involve arbitrary selection, it will be attempted to provide a brief outline of a rather greater number, indicating in particular where they fit into the overall picture and then give detailed references to them in the bibliography at Appendix 2, p 219. To avoid pointless repetition in what follows it will be assumed that the researcher will consult the bibliography for further details of techniques of interest to him.

Figure 5.1 gives an overview of some common purposes of analysis; particular aims consonant with those purposes and certain techniques for meeting those aims.

Purpose	Aim of the analysis	Applicable techniques
Description	Concept formulation	Factor analysis
		Cluster analysis
	Classification	Discriminant analysis
Construction of measurement scales		Regression on surrogate variables
		Unidimensional scaling
		Multidimensional scaling
Generation of empirical relationships	Pattern recognition	Correlation methods
	Derivation of empirical laws	Graphical techniques
Explanation and prediction	Policy analysis	Experimental design model
		Regression model
	Theory building	Path analysis

Figure 5.1   Some common tasks of analysis and techniques applicable to them

TYPES OF DATA AND THEIR PLACE IN ANALYSIS

Before commenting on each of the purposes listed in Figure 5.1 it is useful to review the data typology that will be adopted namely, textual, nominal or categorical, ordinal, interval and ratio. *Textual Data* is the description given to that which records a written or spoken description. Most books and papers are principally composed of material of this kind.

Textual data are rich and flexible but much attention needs to be paid to their content and meaning if they are to be properly understood. Usually they appear in an analysis in summary form as either a precis or as selected quotes. Whilst in some fields, for example biblical studies, concordances exist so that occurrences of particular words or ideas are easily traced, this is not usually the case and hence data of this type can pose particular problems. Although textual data cannot be used directly for quantitative analysis they may form a basis for it. Such analysis is usually referred to as 'content analysis'.

Nominal or *Categorical data* allow classification, for example, 'male', or 'an item of foreign origin'. Such data can be counted and cross tabulated and hence are very frequently used.

Purely nominal data cannot be effectively compared but it is often useful to be able to do this. The first type of data that allows comparison is *ordinal* or *ranked data*. Thus hardness of materials is defined as such a scale by saying material A is harder than material B if it can scratch B. All solid materials can then be ranked in order of increasing hardness on this scale. Note, however, the characteristic feature of such scales in that though A may be harder than B it does not make sense to say A is 1.3 times harder. A type of scale that enables us to measure the differences between individual values on the scale is provided by *Interval data* where an actual numerical value can be given to each point on the scale. Such scales are used for purposes such as the measurement of sound intensity where values are assigned to the difference in intensity of two sounds rather than the absolute intensity of either. Interval scales do not have a meaningful zero although one may be arbitrarily assigned as in the Fahrenheit temperature scale. To obtain *Ratio data* by which individual items can be evaluated on a scale it is necessary for the measurement scale to have a meaningful zero. Many engineering measurements are of this type, for example, length. In the social sciences, too, they occur frequently, for example, national average wage on a particular date.

Any method of quantitative analysis can be applied to ratio data. Most methods can be used with interval data (basically any technique that uses only differences in values). The range of methods that can be applied to ordinal data is considerably smaller whereas with nominal data little can be done besides basic enumeration. As far as quantitative analysis is concerned as we move up the hierarchy from nominal to ratio scales we can extract progressively more from the data. Usually then it is best to obtain the highest level of data one can for analysis.

THE PURPOSE OF ANALYSIS

Having defined the broad framework within which analysis is located the remainder of this chapter will examine each of the major purposes of analysis in turn. The assumption will be that the purpose of the analysis should be a major determinant of the approach used. In general the nearer any technique of analysis is to the bottom of the list in Figure 5.1 the more conditions have to be fulfilled before it can be applied. Many research projects are therefore likely to be concerned with purposes nearer the top of Figure 5.1 particularly those in fields that are relatively little developed so that research is likely to be exploratory rather than explanatory in nature. Furthermore many of the approaches require extended effort and are not suitable for the shorter type of research project. In principle the type of analysis would be decided taking into account these various factors, but in practice there is an addtional significant determinant of the approach, namely the field in which the research is being conducted.

Any subject with a reasonably established tradition will place particular emphasis on certain approaches to analysis. It is hard for instance to conceive of research in physics that would involve purely descriptive analysis based on the use of textual data. In addition it must be remembered that the student will normally need to draw on his supervisor for guidance as to how to conduct his analysis. Obviously this should have some bearing on his choice of approach since otherwise not only may that guidance not be forthcoming but also communication may break down because supervisor and student have no shared language in which to discuss the analysis stage of the project. We can only urge the student to consider how the field in which he is working should affect his approach to analysis, supplemented by the comments made below about general criteria which must be satisfied if logical inferences are to be drawn from analysis.

LOGICAL INFERENCE AND ANALYSIS

The laws of logic constitute 'the rules of the game' that must be observed if the researcher's analysis is to persuade others. Nonetheless it is surprising how often certain basic principles are flouted in the presentation of research findings. For this reason, we would certainly advise the doctoral student to consult some of the texts cited in the bibliography in Appendix 2. Brief comments will be made on some of the more important principles.

Falsifiability

No proposition has value as a basis for research if it cannot be disproved by some data or other. Thus though the suggestion that Sirius is circled by a planet on which live beings who have mastered the art of communicating without using electromagnetic radiation is interesting it is quite unfalsifiable with our existing technology and therefore is not a valid subject for research.

The Need to Search for Alternative Interpretations

Alternative interpretations of data are not normally difficult to find. In a statistical analysis, for example, one that is often very plausible is that the results apparently obtained are 'data artefacts' – merely a function of the particular set of data collected – which would disappear were other data gathered. On the other hand the research student cannot consider every possible alternative. Rather what is required is that he deals with one or two highly plausible ones (especially those that may have been advanced by other researchers) and if his analysis plumps for one of them to justify that decision. By its very nature research work tends to lead to a rather narrow perspective and to find this overturned by a rather obvious oversight at the external examination would be a disaster.

Simplicity of Explanation

Simple explanations are to be preferred to complex ones; valid explanations that involve few variables are superior to those that involve many. Some research fields lend themselves to powerful theories involving only a few basic concepts whereas in others (for example, the social sciences) this is often not the case. However, even in the latter circumstances it is often possible to find one explanation that involves distinctly fewer variables than another. This is frequently a worthwhile aim, since, though an explanation involving very many variables will usually be better for a specific phenomenon it will usually be of far less general applicability.

The Impossibility of Proving Relationships

Outside mathematics the researcher cannot prove explanations or predictions completely, merely render them more probable. For the student the practical implication is that a research project with a demonstrable outcome is often a safer bet than one that attempts to predict or to explain some phenomenon, which in the terminology of Chapter 2 may prove to be highly asymmetrical.

The Need for Variables to Take On More than One Value

If explanation and prediction are to be based on the value of a group of variables it is necessary that those variables be allowed to take on more than one value to demonstrate their effects. Again the practical implications of this are that what can be extracted from the analysis of a particular set of research data depends critically on what variables have taken on more than one value. If it is required to use the value of a particular variable for predictive or explanatory purposes, information about its value must be obtained at the data gathering stage.

Though the need for variables to vary if anything is to be said about their influence may appear self evident it is very common to find unwarranted conclusions being drawn about the influence of variables given the values they have taken.

The foregoing five principles show that the conclusions that can legitimately be derived from an analysis depend critically on the data on which it is based. Any piece of research other than that involving the construction of pure deductive theory, as in mathematics, can be viewed as being based on some type of sample from some notional population. It is often difficult to determine just how the results of a particular study can be generalised if sufficient thought is not given to sample selection prior to data gathering. Accordingly the likelihood of generalising from the results needs to be considered before undertaking the research: a conclusion that will be met again when the problem is examined in the light of the statistical experimental design model later in the chapter.

A REVIEW OF SOME COMMON PURPOSES OF ANALYSIS AND APPLICABLE TECHNIQUES

Description

Description involves a set of activities that are an essential first step in the development of most fields. The student who can indentify a topic about which little is known, of whose importance he can convince others and for which he can collect the data may need to do little other than record them to have his work adjudged satisfactory. Usually, however, knowledge is not so rudimentary and structure must be put on the data by *developing* or *inventing concepts* or *methods of classification*.

1. **Concept Formulation** In order to make any sense of data we need concepts that enable us to focus on those factors and measurements that are relevant to the field of study. In essence a concept is a useful idea with a name and concept formulation is thus intimately associated with the idea of language. A concept to be useful must ideally satisfy a number of criteria. It must be unambiguous so that it is possible for different workers to agree whether or not it applies in any given case. Other workers should find it natural to use and it should be unique and not merely a new name for a concept that already exists in some other field.

Relatively little work seems to have been done on how to effectively formulate concepts from textual data (Bolton 1977). It seems likely, however, that an important method is the use of analogy, for example, the application of the notion of 'half-life', derived from atomic physics, to the declining usefulness of journals with age.

Another very powerful way of developing concepts is the use of pictorial data. The need for the concept of 'crater' in discussing the moon is obvious. In general seeing provides a very powerful way of getting at concepts, for which reasons many statistical approaches present the results in pictorial as well as numerical form.

A variety of statistical methods are available as aids to concept information. These are all based on the underlying notion that good concepts are those which enable us to find differences among the objects under study. They accordingly attempt to tease out the major sources of differences in the data to form prototypes, at least, of useful concepts. The oldest set of statistical techniques are those of *factor analysis*. These take a number of measurements for each object, for example, psychological test scores and attempt to select from them a few combinations of these measurements that explain most of the differences between individuals; the so-called 'factors', which can then be named. This approach has been applied in intelligence testing to identify the factors of spatial ability and verbal ability.

Another approach is to compare objects according to how similar they are and then group them in descending order of similarity. This is the basis of *cluster analysis*. Thus we might consider grouping people in the light of similarities in educational qualifications. A number of groups would then be expected to emerge naturally, for example, those educated to postgraduate level, to graduate level, to A level, and so on.

2. Classification The successful development of concepts results in a number of 'pigeon holes' into which individual objects can be classified.

The easiest type of classification procedure to adopt is one that assesses each of the objects to be classified in the light of the concepts to be applied and then assigns it to the category which it most nearly fits. Thus someone who spends ten hours a week playing football for no financial reward might be assigned to the category 'amateur footballer' rather than 'professional footballer' if the concepts relevant to this classification decision are 'hours spent playing football' and 'whether paid'. An obvious refinement of this idea is to weight the different concepts according to their importance. Subjective weighting schemes of this type are frequently employed, for example, in market research (cf. Churchman *et al.*, 1957).

Rather than derive the weightings subjectively it is often useful to calculate them using the statistical technique known as *discriminant analysis*. The essence of the approach is simple: a number of objects that have already been classified are taken. Measurements of a number of variables for each of them are used to set up a set of predictor functions that will enable future cases to be classified by using a weighted combination of the relevant measurements.

Construction of Measurement Scales

A frequent purpose of analysis is the construction of a measurement scale of the interval or ratio type; such a need occurs surprisingly often. For example, a host of different variables such as height and weight, can be measured for a building but none of them provides a direct measurement of the attribute 'earthquakeproofness'.

Traditionally the approach to the problem of constructing scales has been to adopt surrogate measures for example, the use of performance on standard flame tests, as a measure of fire resistance. During the past thirty years however a host of techniques have been developed by psychologists in particular, for constructing scales for which no 'obvious' measurement exists. These may be single (univariate) scales which measure a variable along a single dimension, for example, the measurement of an 'intelligence quotient'. On the other hand multidimensional scaling techniques apply to situations where more than one concept, or dimension, is relevant. In the case of two dimensions such techniques result in a 'perceptual map'. To revert to our earlier example of the footballer it might well be that in this case it might be sensible to measure interest in football along two dimensions: a) the average hours per week spent playing football; b) the proportion of the individual's income derived from football. Such a graph would obviously provide a richer measure of the variable of interest than a univariate scale.

Generating Empirical Relationships

This section is concerned with the identification of regularities and relationships amongst data. This is an area in which the research student can often expect the major results of his analysis to fall. Whilst the sciences and engineering pay considerable attention to the derivation of empirical laws this is less so in the social sciences and humanities. Relatively little seems to have been published on suitable techniques. All in all this area seems underrepresented in texts on research methodology, given its importance in much student research and for this reason will be explored at some length here.

The essence of the problems dealt with in this section is that there is usually no obvious idea of what relationship will be found and the richness of the data need to be displayed in such a way as to suggest fruitful avenues to explore; pictures often provide a good way of doing this. Since pictorial approaches are often considerably facilitated by automatic plotting and most institutions now have access to a computer graph plotter, it may well be worth the student exploring the use of a suitable computer graphics package (see Chapter 8).

1. Pattern Recognition The recognition of pattern and order in data is a fundamental step in the development of theories to explain them. Patterns may conveniently be broken down into three basic types: those showing association among variables, those showing groupings and those showing order or precedence relationships between variables.

a) Association   Association between two variables is very easily detected using a scatter diagram in which one variable is plotted against another. The quantitative equivalent of a scatter diagram is the correlation coefficient, for which, there is, of course, an extensive statistical theory.

Equivalents of the simple correlation coefficient exist for the case where there are more than two variables. A useful measure is the partial correlation coefficient that measures the strength of association between two variables when the effects of another variable on both of them are allowed for. This is useful, for instance, in cases of spurious correlation such as the relationship between the number of US pigs and US output of pig iron both of which are substantially associated with the third variable, US gross national product per head. Partial correlation methods are in turn closely related to those of path analysis, discussed later.

b) Grouping techniques   These are obviously closely related to the classification problem discussed earlier. In the present case however, our interest is in situations in which the number of classifications (if any) is unknown. For this reason methods such as cluster analysis are appropriate whereas discriminant analysis is not.

c) Precedence relationships   A type of pattern that occurs in many different contexts is that which shows order, precedence or priority. Perhaps the simplest instance is one where we search for a pattern in some sequence of activities, for example, in detecting a 'typical' pattern of community growth from hamlet to city.

The quantitative approach to detecting sequences of this type is by the use of cross correlation coefficients that measure the strength of the relationship between one variable and another a specified number of time units later. They are much used in econometrics and in control engineering for detecting the lag between a change in one variable, and the corresponding change in another, for example, an upsurge in orders and the consequent upsurge in deliveries.

2. Derivation of Empirical Laws In many fields of technology it is possible to develop empirical laws in the form of simple equations relating one interval or ratio scaled variable to a few others. Since it is generally possible to find simple relationships between variables there is a long tradition of using graphical methods for their determination particularly where detailed theoretical knowledge is lacking. Such laws are of considerable practical use in engineering, and for researchers in associated fields. To them the methods described may well be very familiar. In the main, however, the picture has been very different in the social sciences. The general belief has been that there is no reason to expect that relationships between variables will be simple and therefore there is scant point in trying to establish them using graphical techniques.

Ehrenberg (1975) has argued forcefully that a great deal more could and should be done in this direction by social scientists, and accordingly this section is primarily intended for researchers in this field. It is perhaps worth beginning by suggesting why simple laws can be found in the physical sciences and the circumstances under which it might be worthwhile looking for them in the social sciences. Basically simple relationships seem attainable in the physical sciences because they typically describe the behaviour of many millions of entities, for example, where we relate the maximum safe load on an embankment, comprising billions of molecules, to the angle its sides make with the horizontal. This suggests that success in finding simple empirical laws in the social sciences is most likely in fields where the behaviour of a very large number of objects is being described. Thus, as an example, in a number of countries the proportion of companies above a certain size, as measured by turnover or manpower, can be well described by a standard statistical distribution known as the Pareto distribution. This is an excellent example of how a large population (several hundred thousand in the UK) can exhibit considerable regularity.

Searching for empirical relationships is best done using certain tricks of the trade. By far the most important are the use of various types of scale that lead to straight line graphs, since a straight line relationship is much easier to fit by eye and lends itself to unambiguous extrapolation. The starting point of any study of relationships between two variables then will be the graphing of Variable A against Variable B on simple linear scales, that is, the construction of a scatter diagram. If a reasonable straight line fit is found no more need be done. Otherwise the next step must be to apply nonlinear scales to one or both variables. Graph papers are available with a variety of different scales. Indeed a glance at the catalogue of a specialist supplier can itself be a useful way of deciding possible nonlinear relationships to explore.

Explanation and Prediction

Traditionally in the Anglo Saxon world knowledge and research have been equated with the identification of causal relationships and research directed to this end has been accorded the highest esteem. Many fields have not yet been developed to the level where causal explanation is possible or valid predictions can be made. These offer their own special research opportunities as has already been discussed. Nonetheless where sufficient knowledge exists to make explanation or prediction possible it is not easy to see what benefits would be attained if they were not attempted. In this sense explanation and prediction must be seen as involving a higher level of knowledge – though, of course, not necessarily a higher level of research skill.

The meaning of the notions of 'cause' and 'causality' have exercised philosophers for at least three centuries and continue to be the subject of lively debate. Experience suggests that whereas epistemological considerations of this type are usually too time consuming for the researcher involved in a short project, the student undertaking a research degree will often find it necessary to give thought to these matters at some stage in his work. Since the space required to adequately rehearse the philosophical arguments would be substantial the interested reader is referred to the bibliography at Appendix 2. For the purpose of discussion however it is necessary to give a more concrete interpretation to the idea of establishing causal relationships. In practice this involves the interrelated activities of explanation and prediction which are often couched in terms of hypotheses, for example, 'the existence of a close knit Quaker community was an important factor in the early development of the iron industry' (implicit explanation) or 'the tumbling costs of computer hardware have made software costs a more important factor in developing a computer system' (implicit prediction). Since most tests of hypotheses[1] appear to fall into one or other of these categories and the logical and statistical methods required are the same as those needed for explanation and prediction, they will not be discussed independently.

In what follows explanation and prediction will be construed as enabling the values of one set of variables to be derived given the values of another. Thus the biochemist may direct his efforts to explaining why the body rejects certain types of foreign tissue. Better explanations of tissue rejection in turn enable better predictions to be made about the likelihood of rejection given various forms of treatment. Equally an important test of a theory is that it makes predictions which can be confirmed by observation or experiment. In pure science then explanation and prediction are intermingled. In fields such as engineering this may also be the case but the fact that research is often directed towards the formulation of empirical laws on which predictions can be based means that there also exists the possibility of successful prediction for which no satisfactory explanation can be given. Thus in hydraulics it is possible to apply standard formulae to relate the flow of a river to its gradient and depth but to give a satisfactory explanation of the basis of the formulae may not be possible. This type of situation illustrates another facet of the interrelationship between explanation and prediction. That is that, in practice, we often

---

1. By 'tests of hypotheses' in this context the evaluation of the credibility of some hypotheses like those above is meant and not the narrower definition employed in elementary statistics.

use the same method for testing out whether we can satisfactorily predict a phenomenon as we do to establish whether we can successfully explain it.

In many social sciences explanation is often deemed impossible because of the complexity of the systems involved. Frequently the task of social sciences is, therefore, presented as finding associations between variables that can be generalised to various situations, for example, that urbanisation leads to a growth in reported crimes. Though a variety of explanations of this phenomenon have been offered by criminologists, sociologists, and so forth, none can be said to command general acceptance. Nonetheless such an association is useful, if it can be established, because it forms the basis of prediction.

Some research students find themselves working in the broad area of *policy analysis*. The aim of their research is either to carry out an evaluation of the effects of past policies and draw lessons from it (evaluation research) or to formulate, and argue the case for, new policies. Much social science research is of this type as, less obviously, is a considerable amount of research in technology. What differentiates this type of research from those discussed hitherto is that it is primarily aimed at non-academic audiences. Nevertheless, though it has an obvious 'political' dimension it must still meet academic standards and since such research clearly involves explanation and prediction the relevant standards are those pertaining to those topics.

Several techniques which are relevant to explanation and prediction will be examined briefly. As indicated in Figure 5.1 these are experimental design, regression, and path analysis.

1. **The Experimental Design Model** Aside from its applicability in analysing many different types of research data the experimental design model has considerable virtues as a conceptual model of research directed towards explanation and prediction.

Fundamental to the model is the notion that the variable of interest can be measured on a ratio or interval scale and that the values of the variable to be explained or predicted are affected by a number of other variables usually referred to as factors. Each factor takes on more than one value and each value is called a factor level. Factors may often however be measured on nominal scales, for example, fertilizer A, fertilizer B, or represent fairly crude groupings, for example, application of less than 100 grams of fertilizer per square metre; application greater than 100 grams per square metre, and so on. Finally we assume that for each combination of factor levels we have at least one measurement of the variable whose value is to be explained or predicted. The model assumes this value is made up of a number of components: a base value plus various additive effects due to each of the factor levels and also due to interactions between factor levels, plus finally a random term representing errors in measurements, the effects of factors not considered directly and so on.

The virtues of the experimental design model as a conceptual model of the processes involved in explanation and prediction are very considerable even if, for whatever reason, no attempt is made to carry out a statistical analysis. It offers an explanatory framework which is capable of handling complex relationships between the respondent variables and factor levels along with predictions of the effect of any particular set of factor levels. The factor levels can be recognised as independent variables and the implicit requirement of the model that there be at least two levels of each factor enables their effects to be isolated. The experimental design model assumes that the researcher can control the experiment to the extent of selecting the factors and factor levels whose effects are to be examined. This is, of course, not always the case in the social sciences but it may still be possible to approximate to an experimental design by using the fact that particular variables vary between one organisation or country and another or over time. Such applications of the model are usually referred to as 'quasi-experiments' (Campbell and Stanley, 1966).

2. **The Regression Model** The attraction of the regression model is that it deals with situations where there is no control over the selection of factor levels. In principle, it expresses a dependent variable y in terms of various independent variables x_1, x_2, and so on, the precise form of the relationship being derived from the data. Obviously this model represents a generalisation of the experimental design model since the x's can represent combinations of factor levels/treatments and may be nominal, interval or ratio data. The particular advantage of the regression model is that it does not require observations to be available for specific factor combinations and to a large extent, then, it is capable of utilising the data 'as they are'. On the other hand this usually means that the rigorous control implicit in experimental design is lost and so the researcher cannot always have the same faith in his results as when an experimental design approach is feasible.

3. **Path Analysis** Another model that is related to the regression model is that of path analysis. In essence this attempts to select the set of relationships between variables that is most consistent with the available data. As such it has an obvious bearing on the problem of distinguishing independent, dependent and intermediate variables. As a typical exam-

ple we might consider two possible explanations for the strong correlation between father's social status and son's social status that is observed in many western countries. The simple explanation is that the father's status determines the son's status directly. A less obvious explanation is that the father's determines the level to which the son is educated and the level of the son's education determines his status. Path analysis enables a choice to be made between such competing hypotheses on the basis of survey data.

TESTING A QUANTITATIVE ANALYSIS

Until now this chapter has been concerned with statistical methods mainly as models of particular types of analysis. For statistical methods of analysis it is, of course, possible to specify procedures for testing results derived from them. Since there are very considerable overlaps in testing procedures for different statistical methods discussion of this question has been delayed to this point. The most common reasons for the rejection of a piece of research are: a) lack of depth and b) faulty analysis. The first problem has already been covered through our review of common types of analysis. The second relates to inadequate testing of his conclusions by the researcher, typically an optimistic assessment of the degree to which his data and analysis support the hypotheses he advances. As such it reflects insufficient attention to the quality of his results, which in turn shows ineffective management of a key aspect of the research project. For this reason and because this subject is not so well covered in the literature as are statistical methods, this topic is now examined further. Most statistical techniques embody methods of testing the results they give for statistical significance. In practice, however, such tests often given an overly rosy picture of the results obtained from them. Basically this is because the test must be based on the notion that some statistical model or other describes reality perfectly, whereas, at best it describes it only imperfectly. It is, therefore, useful, particularly where more complex models are concerned, to supplement the statistical tests with other ways of evaluating the results of an analysis. A number of strategies for testing an analysis, namely, complete enumeration, checking for representativeness, random split half methods, hold out methods, checking for missing explanatory variables will be discussed.

Complete Enumeration

As observed earlier most research involves (notional) sampling and hence sampling error. One strategy available to some researchers however is that of complete enumeration – a census. Thus many studies of UK companies are restricted to those that are listed on the Stock Exchange, since as far as published accounting data are concerned complete enumeration of the couple of thousand companies involved is perfectly realistic where it would not be if the study were to cover the several hundred thousand unlisted companies also.

Checking for Representativeness

As is evident from any textbook, statistical theory relies heavily on the notion of random samples. A frequently adopted procedure for assessing the randomness of a sample is to check how representative it is by comparison with information known about the population being sampled from other sources. Thus in a study of corrosion problems in cars the number of cars of each make and year in the sample could be compared with what might be expected on the basis of information about the actual numbers of cars in each category in the UK as recorded at the Vehicle Licensing Office in Swansea. Often several characteristics can be checked in this way. Thus it would also be possible to check the number of vehicle owners in each social class in the sample against the Registrar General's estimates for the population as a whole.

This type of approach has obvious links with the device of quota sampling much used in market research.

Reliability – Random Split Half Testing

Scale construction can often run into significant problems of reproduction, in that aspects of the scales are very much a figment of the data used and disappear if other data are studied. In essence this problem is due to an attempt to overexplain the preferences or attitudes being scaled, A useful way of detecting the problem is to split the data randomly into two halves and to carry out the scaling operations on each completely separately. If the two samples give similar results they are combined and the analysis carried out again on the total sample. Where they give different results attempts should be made to eliminate the problem by simplification, for example, by reducing the number of dimensions in multi-dimensional scaling.

Usually data can be split randomly several times and the procedure repeated with a consequent increase in the reliability of the results. Random split half methods are well suited to tests of factor analyses, scales, and cluster analyses, and to the evaluation of discriminant functions and regression models. Their biggest drawback is that large amounts of data are required. The sample size usually recommended for cluster analysis, for example, is of the order of several hundred if split half techniques are to be used.

Hold Out Methods

Where fewer data are available hold out methods are often attractive. The essence of such a method is to remove the data from one (or a few) object(s) or respondent(s) and derive the scale, discriminant function, and so on using the remaining data and then with the model obtained compute the relevant values for the held out data and use these to evaluate the performance of the function in question. Thus in testing a regression model to be based on n observations, one is removed at random and the model computed on the basis of the other n–1. This model is then used to predict the value of the dependent variable for the held out data point from the values of its independent variables.

Hold out methods are obviously closely related to testing through prediction and the connection in many cases between prediction and satisfactory explanation has already been discussed. In practice the hold out process is repeated a number of times and each of the resulting models are compared. Where the removal of one or a few data points causes a marked change in the model it is a clear sign that the analysis is far from satisfactory. Again simplification may often resolve the problem, for example reduction of the number of independent variables on which a discriminant function is based. For small data sets in particular, hold out methods are an excellent safeguard against an apparent, though in fact spurious, high degree of success in fitting the model in question.

In certain fields, such as econometrics, a slightly different approach is possible. Thus a regression model can be constructed using data for the period 1970-79 and tested on data for 1980. This reflects the fact that *extrapolation*, that is prediction for values of the independent variable outside the data set, is always a more powerful test than *interpolation* where the prediction is made for a value within the original data set.

Checking for missing Explanatory Variables

Sometimes bias may be introduced into the analysis because important explanatory variables have been omitted. Thus a study aimed at increasing the amount of time certain equipment is productive where the users were recruited on a voluntary basis might well result in a preponderance of users whose equipment spends an above average proportion of time out of service. In this case the relevant measure of bias would be the average proportion of time the user's equipment is out of service. In such cases the bias can either be reduced or removed by using this variable as a factor in an experimental design model or by formally accounting for its effects through a regression equation. This latter approach is often used, for example, in the assessment of training programmes where participants are given a pre-test and a post-test on a relevant area of knowledge so that the impact of prior learning on the effect of the training can be established.

Another approach to this problem that is useful in longitudinal studies conducted over a period of time is to use time itself as one of the dependent variables. Where it turns out to be an important explanatory variable this is usually a sign that other important dependent variables that have changed in a systematic way with time have been omitted from the study. A similar approach often adopted in studies of organisations is to use some measure of size as an additional variable of same type.

THE USE OF THE COMPUTER IN ANALYSIS

If the researcher wishes to use many of the techniques discussed here as distinct from merely viewing them as providing a conceptual model of some type of analysis, then he will not only need to be familiar with the underlying theory of these methods but also he will need to use a computer program to carry out the analysis. There is no doubt that the advent of large statistical computer packages, in particular, has made a considerable difference to what the present generation of research students can expect to do by way of quantitative analysis, compared with what was feasible for their supervisors. In our view this is a fact to be taken into account when deciding on the worth of the analysis contained in a research report or thesis. What might previously have been regarded as desirable but infeasible, is now straightforward for the student who has mastered the use of the computer. If this is the case (and there are of course still research projects where it is not) then it seems only reasonable that the student be expected to carry out the necessary computer analysis. Under those circumstances this needs to be taken into account at the stage of planning the research, since, even if the student already possesses the requisite computing knowledge, it will almost certainly have an impact of the way data are gathered and recorded.

ENSURING THE ANALYSIS IS OF AN APPROPRIATE STANDARD

There are many aspects to analysis and even the somewhat cursory discussion here has necessarily been fairly long. It is worth, therefore, recapitulating the opening remarks. An acceptable analysis is in many ways the key aspect of any research study and the student who wishes to manage his research effectively must accordingly ensure that his analysis is adequate. It may be helpful to bear the following points in mind:

1. Plan the analysis early in the project so that data gathering can be organised around it and any necessary skills can be acquired.
2. Make sure that you are thoroughly familiar with the methods of analysis usually employed in your field of study, particularly if you wish to deviate from them.
3. Decide on the methods to be used and master the relevant literature particularly that dealing with the snags and pitfalls.
4. Where possible, make the analysis quantitative. Do not avoid employing an appropriate method, for example, a computer package, just because it will require time to learn it. Do not on the other hand, lavish sophisticated techniques on data of dubious quality. Data can be poor and no amount of analysis can put that right.
5. Make sure that the analysis respects the rules of logical inference given above.
6. Test your conclusions wherever possible using the methods suggested in the literature and in this chapter.
7. Write down conclusions as you go so it is clear what you are claiming. Expose them to the scrutiny of your supervisor and your friends. Review them every month or so as the analysis progresses to make sure they stand the test of time.
8. Where doubts are expressed about either the logic of your conclusions, or whether the analysis has the necessary depth for your

level of research, heed them. If nothing more, they show that there is at least one person who is unconvinced about an important aspect of your research.

9. Try to do rather more than is necessary. An analysis that aims at minimum standards all the way through not only runs a considerable risk of rejection by the examiners, it is also unsatisfying to the researcher and means that he loses much of the benefit he should have derived from carrying out his research.

SUMMARY

> THE ROLE OF ANALYSIS: is to supply evidence which
> justifies claims that the research changes belief or
> knowledge and is of sufficient value. This is done through
> the ordering or structuring of data.

> THE DIRECT PURPOSES OF ANALYSIS: are description,
> construction of measurement scales, generation of
> empirical relationships, and explanation and prediction.

> ANALYSIS TO BE CONVINCING: must satisfy the
> principles of logical inference.

> QUANTITATIVE ANALYSES MAY BE TESTED: by a
> number of techniques besides those usually given in
> statistics texts.

> COMPUTER KNOWLEDGE: is increasingly being required
> for analysis and this trend is unlikely to be reversed.

6

Gathering the Data

Almost all research projects involve the gathering of data. Indeed, as remarked earlier, that process is often equated with research itself. As a key activity in a research project data gathering must be managed and this has two aspects. On the one hand there is a technical component concerned with why data are collected and how to do so. On the other there are a variety of tasks connected with successful data gathering which must be carried out effectively.

Chapter 5 shows that the type of analysis employed and its purpose substantially dictate the types of data needed. In practice however many types of analysis and therefore of research project are difficult or impossible to carry out because suitable data gathering techniques are not available. The invention of new methods of collecting data or the improvement of existing ones can therefore have a substantial impact on the research done in a particular field. At the higher levels of research just as the development of new methods of analysis is often a good route to success so, too, is introduction of novel approaches to data gathering or of major refinements to techniques already in use.

It is useful in the present context to recognise two categories: primary data which the researcher collects himself through observation, experiment, and so on and secondary data that have been collected by others. The gathering of secondary data often has much in common with literature searching and many of the techniques of Chapter 4 apply here. Furthermore data acquired from the literature search whether they consist of measurements by other workers or statements of opinions and theories is often the major source of data for fields such as theoretical physics or philosophy where at first sight research can be conducted without data.

Whether the researcher is concerned with primary or secondary data there are a number of general points that apply to either type and these will be discussed before considering the individual types of data in more detail.

ACTIVITIES INVOLVED IN DATA GATHERING

However the researcher chooses to collect his data certain activities will be common. The data must be located and arrangements made for their collection. They must be collected; recorded in a form suitable for the intended analysis and checked. Adjustments may then need to be made for errors and omissions or data that for some reason are unusable.

The location of data may often be very difficult and at higher levels the researcher is, at the outset, often unsure as to what his sources will be. Against that data for the short term research project need to be fairly accessible if the data gathering stage of the project is not to get out of hand. Students undertaking short projects must avoid situations where a great deal of effort is involved in arranging the data collection because, for example, laboratory rigs have to be set up and commissioned, or because considerable training is needed before a particular data collection method can be used.

The gathering of data requires time and there are relatively few fields in which it does not also involve substantial effort. On occasions it may be necessary to await rather infrequent events as in a study of volcanic eruptions, or the actual process of obtaining the measurements may be long drawn out as in certain biomedical tests. Whatever is involved in gathering the data, the process by which they are recorded often sets a definite limit on the rate at which they can be gathered and the ease with which they can be analysed. It is no accident that the fields in which most data are gathered, such as radio astronomy, are almost totally dependent on computer methods for gathering and recording data.

In short data gathering requires time: for acquiring skills and making the necessary arrangements for collection and to ensure adequate quality, and time is usually the researcher's major resource. Furthermore it is affected by technology which may place definite restrictions on what can be done in collecting and recording data.

ACCESS TO DATA

Gaining access to data is often a problem for the student researcher. He may need to use special facilities where application to use them must be made long in advance and which may be rationed in other ways. The social scientist often finds that the organisations or groups that he wishes to study are unwilling for reasons of confidentiality or lack of time to provide him with data.

The student who is involved in a short research project cannot afford such problems and if access to data is difficult he should find another project. In the longer project, however, where the student is willing to contemplate a period of negotiation it is worth bearing in mind a number of devices for improving his chances of getting access to the data he needs.

Firstly, the sponsorship of a prestigious institution and/or of some individual of distinction is extremely useful. Research students are fortunate in that educational institutions do still enjoy high prestige and if the student is sponsored or supported by an official body, this may well be of great benefit in obtaining access.

In broad terms co-operation is, of course, most likely where the provider of access gains something in return. If the results of the work are of interest to him then promise of a copy of any papers that emerge from it may help to secure collaboration. Also, as observed in Chapter 4 many types of data are a tradeable commodity and the researcher may be able to gain access on condition that he makes his data available once collected. The researcher has, of course, a responsibility to later researchers. He should observe the elementary politenesses and as far as possible adhere to any bargains that may be struck so that, for example, if a copy of the research report is promised this should be provided.

GATHERING DATA TO AN ADEQUATE STANDARD

In our view it is important that the researcher demonstrates that his data were properly collected. Ideally this means that others would have been able to arrive at the same readings or observations as he obtained. Where primary data are concerned this is usually not feasible. Instead he must settle for following a procedure that will be adjudged adequate in the light of the level of his research; in particular by the examiner to whom the research project will be sent for assessment. This question is taken up later in the broader context of the assessment of the research report. Here, however discussion will be confined to a checklist of points intended to secure adequate data gathering standards and which applies to secondary as well as primary data. These are that:

1. the data actually measure what they purport to measure;
2. proper attention was paid to measurement error and the reduction of its effects;
3. a suitable sample was used, in particular that a) it provided a basis for generalisation and that b) it was large enough for the effects of interest to be detected;
4. data were properly recorded, in particular that a) the conditions under which the data were gathered were properly noted and that b) suitable data recording methods were used and efforts were made to detect and eliminate errors arising during recording.

Not all of these points apply in every situation, and the full list is perhaps only appropriate in the, albeit common, situation where data are to be gathered in some systematic way and are of the nominal, ordinal, interval or ratio type. The researcher's own notes which we view as textual data and an important data source, would probably need to be judged only against standard 4. Nonetheless the list will now be reviewed point by point, with the greatest emphasis being placed on data recording

Ensuring the Data Measure what they Purport to Measure

In the last chapter it was noted that very often it is difficult to measure the actual variable of interest and instead surrogate measures may be adopted. This is particularly likely to be a problem in secondary data gathering where the researcher may not know just how the data were derived. For instance, there is at least one country whose smooth upward growth in recorded consumption data over the 1970s probably owes more to the predilections of the civil servant who calculates them than to the behaviour of consumption itself.

Errors in Measurement

Quantitative data are often subject to measurement error and the size of that error may have important implications for both the way the data are used and for the scale of the data gathering effort.

Aside from errors due to malfunction of measuring equipment which are of no interest in this context, error may take the form of bias, as in the underreporting of small company activities in many official statistics; deliberate or instinctive falsehood, as in many answers to questionnaire surveys; or distortion of one form of another as in the response of a laboratory amplifier to a high frequency signal. The practical implication of all three possibilities is the same: information is lost and the data do not fully represent the phenomenon under study. Though it is often easier for the engineer to overcome such difficulties by employing more sophisticated measuring devices similar opportunities may well arise in the social sciences. Webb *et al.* (1966) make a number of creative suggestions for methods of coping with this problem in the social sciences, by the device of 'unobtrusive measurement' for example, measuring the popularity of paintings in art galleries by wear on carpets in their vicinity.

Another form of measurement error that is relevant to quantitative data is pure random error that is supposed on average to fluctuate about zero. Since this is relatively easy to cope with statistically, it is the usual (though not always the most accurate) model of error adopted.

In practice we can attempt to deal with measurement error in one of two ways. One is to measure the phenomenon of interest by two different methods. Where each gives rise to random measurement error a combination of the two measurements can be expected to give a better estimate of the true value provided the two methods are not subject to the same error. Obviously this approach requires more data gathering effort.

The alternative way of dealing with measurement error that is more or less random is to increase the size of the sample and this is discussed below.

Choosing the Sample

Data gathering normally involves some kind of sampling and the conclusions that can validly be drawn from that sample depend critically on both the population sampled and the procedures used for generating the sample. The first step in choosing the sample is accordingly to choose a target population to be sampled that permits interesting conclusions to be drawn and to select a sample in such a way that the conclusions are valid. Though this is unlikely to be a problem for the physical scientist it certainly is in many other fields particularly the social sciences. Very often the sheer cost of data gathering pushes the student in the direction of some 'convenience sample' that meets neither of these criteria.

Any statistical method requires a certain size of sample to have a reasonable probability of detecting an effect of interest and in these circumstances the collection of enough data may be quite beyond the resources available to the student researcher. Some social science projects, for example, are very unlikely to produce the hoped for results because they are not based on enough observations. Thus the effects of positive discrimination programmes such as educational priority areas may be difficult to measure because they are swamped by environmental variables that have a far greater impact. In such cases a large sample is needed if the effects are to be revealed. A crude rule of thumb applicable in a number of situations is that the sample size needed is proportional to the square of the accuracy of the estimates derived from the sample. Thus to double the accuracy it is necessary to increase the sample size fourfold. It follows that the ideas of statistical power testing that enable the necessary sample size to be inferred before carrying out the data gathering are likely to be of much interest to the student researcher (cf. Cohen, 1969).

There are many different procedures that can be used for sampling and the reader should consult a specialist text, for example, Som (1973) for further details.

Recording the Data

In Chapter 5 the relevance of the experimental design model to many types of research was discussed. An important aspect of that model is the idea of factors and, by implication at least, the values of all factor levels should be recorded along with the actual measurements of interest. This provides protection against the discovery that further variables, and therefore, measurements, are relevant to the phenomenon in question. Equally, notes on the sources of data, and time and date of collection can be extremely useful when many months later the researcher is attempting to correct an error or to decide whether a set of figures whose origin he has long since forgotten can be used in analysis. Clearly in both cases the recording of adequate additional information will help to ensure that few data that have been collected will prove to be unusable. Experience suggests that this is by no means always the case. Researchers do waste effort by having to repeat data gathering activities because certain information was omitted originally. In practice it is almost always straightforward to collect additional measurements, and so on, when the initial data gathering takes place. In further discussions of data recording it will, therefore, be assumed that consideration has been given to exactly what measurements, and so on, need to be recorded and the focus now will be on how to record them.

In primary data gathering recording may involve two processes. Firstly, data must be captured in some way that is feasible in the context in which they are to be gathered, following which it is often necessary to transcribe or convert the data into a form suited to computer input.

Transcription may, of course, be needed even when the computer is not used, for example, when a typed record of an interview is required. The main concern here, however, is the reduction of data to a form suitable for computer analysis. Ratio and interval scaled data are already in this form and present no problem. Ordinal data can either be input as ranks or equivalently using letter codes, for example, $A = 1$, $B = 2$. Pictorial data need to be converted into numbers in some way or other. Nominal data may be recorded by using 1 to denote the presence of some attribute, for example, the item is green, or zero if it does not possess it. For pure textual data there is little choice but to input them as they stand.

Transcription may also be the major process involved when secondary data are being used. This two stage process is at best somewhat inefficient and at worst may introduce errors at the transcription stage, so automatic data gathering methods that collect the data directly in a form suitable for computer analysis have obvious attractions.

The detection of errors at the data capture stage may, by analogy with data processing terminology by dubbed *validation*. The ensuring of accurate transcription will similarly be referred to as *verification*.

Validation is primarily based on identifying implausible data, for example, a questionnaire that records a pregnant man or more typically but more subtly one anomalous liberal response from an individual amidst a host of authoritarian ones. Not all such anomalies will, in fact, be errors and conversely such procedures will not identify data that could be correct but in fact are not. Successful validation is heavily dependent on experience and this is one reason why training in the use of data gathering techniques is necessary.

Verification lends itself to more mechanical methods. The traditional approach in data processing, for example, is for two different people to enter the same data into the computer system and then accept the two sets of data if they are the same but otherwise to examine them for transcription errors. This approach relies on the reasonable assumption that the same mistake is unlikely to be made by two different individuals.

The rejection of data at the validation or verification stage is a somewhat negative process. Though transcription errors are usually remediable, validation errors will not be unless thought is given to making them so. The only way in which this can be done is to introduce redundancy – that is, extra information – into the data gathered so that incorrect or missing data can be reconstructed. If, for instance, the aim is to measure a length the simplest way is to measure it in say millimetres and record it. If this is done incorrectly however the complete set of measurements related to this length will have to be thrown away. On the other hand if it is also measured in inches it will be possible to determine the true length if validation checks cast doubt on the recorded figure for the length in millimetres. This example also throws light on the role of 'feel' in validation. Most people in the UK have a far better intrinsic concept of imperial measurements than metric ones and a check of this sort will accordingly have a high chance of detecting the error at the time when the measurement is made.

In many social science applications it may well be possible to approach the respondents again and in science and engineering studies the measurements can, in principle, be repeated. Nonetheless both of these require effort and in some cases may for all practical purposes be impossible. Therefore if the researcher is to avoid throwing away hard won data he is well advised to devote a little thought to how errors in them can be detected and eliminated. Accordingly he may well find it worthwhile to consult a standard reference on data processing for further details of relevant techniques (for example, Yeates, 1971).

Though the avoidance of error is a common theme in all types of data capture or transcription there are many different methods that can be used for either or both of these purposes. These differ in the amount of equipment and preparation required to use them, in their costs and in their suitability for dealing with large volumes of data. Though the division is far from being clear cut it is useful to distinguish between methods that are primarily suited to data capture and those that are mainly used for transcription, and that approach will be followed here.

a) Data Capture

Figure 6.1 lists some common methods of data capture. As, with increasing frequency, the data will be subjected to computer analysis the methods are divided into two groups according to whether transcription is needed and range from 'traditional' methods requiring subsequent transcription through to sophisticated ones that cut out this latter process

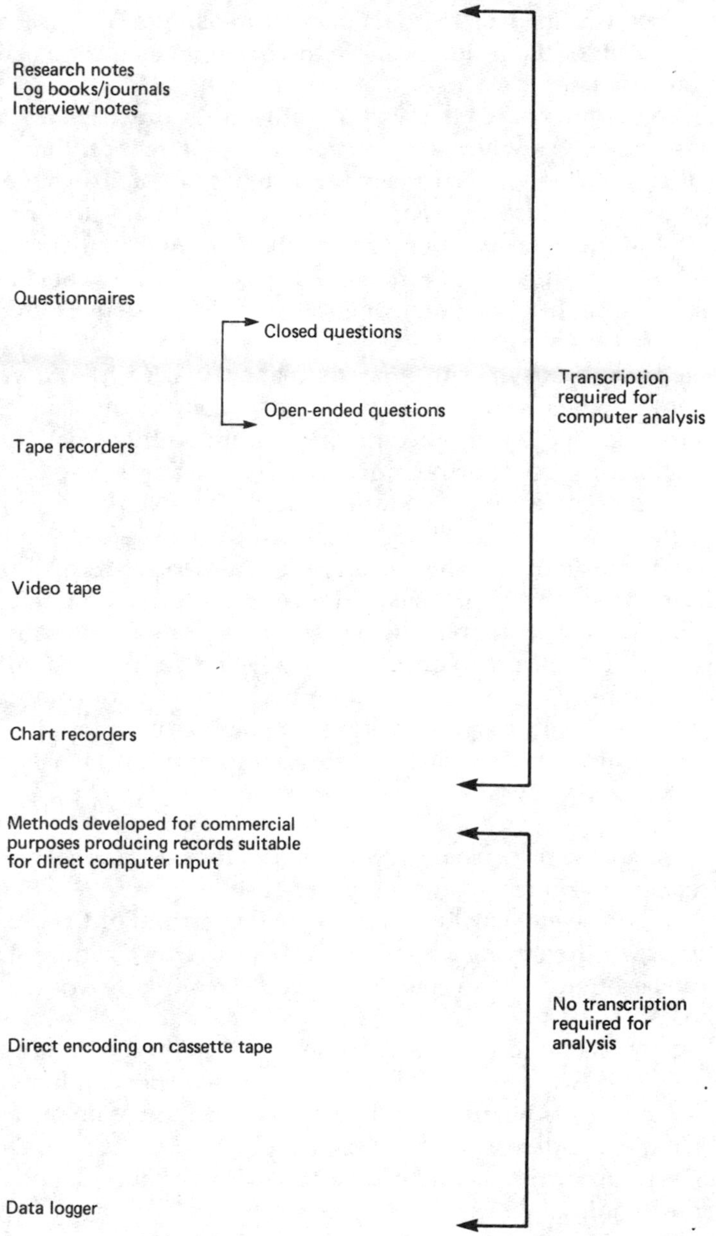

Research notes
Log books/journals
Interview notes

Questionnaires

→ Closed questions

→ Open-ended questions

Tape recorders

Transcription
required for
computer analysis

Video tape

Chart recorders

Methods developed for commercial
purposes producing records suitable
for direct computer input

No transcription
required for
analysis

Direct encoding on cassette tape

Data logger

Figure 6.1 Some common methods of data capture

at the cost of much greater dependence on equipment. The initial discussion will be confined to the data recording aspects of these methods though certain of them, for example, questionnaires will be considered more broadly later.

The one form of data that will be gathered by any researcher are his own research notes which are worthy of more attention than they are often afforded. Though the researcher who has pursued an almost uninterrupted academic career should have developed effective notetaking practice this may need amendment when, as is often the case, his research is concerned with a new field of study. The problems of the part-time researcher or of someone returning to academic study after a number of years are likely to be greater.

The basic problem with notes is that they arise from a variety of activities from the researcher's own reading through to occasional flashes of inspiration. Usually they eventually comprise a huge mass of data of many different types. Furthermore there is no simple way of ensuring that two different pieces of data that should be juxtaposed will be.

As far as notes on books are concerned the most effective practice is probably to make them as the books are read and to produce Xerox copies of selected passages of particular interest that can be annotated as the student wishes. The annotations should rarely amount to more than a few per cent of the work in question unless some form of textual study is being undertaken, so there should be no problem with copyright law. Certainly it is usually a sign that the researcher has not properly digested the contents of a work if he finds it necessary to copy most of it and proper cross-referencing soon becomes impossible if the practice is repeated wholesale.

Normally the researcher will want to produce substantial notes of his own relating to projected analyses, organisation of the research report and so on. These are usually more easy to deal with. For the unexpected insight it is worth carrying a small pocket book in which sufficient information can be jotted down to enable the idea to be properly worked up later into notes.

Log books and journals are the simplest method of data recording available to the experimental scientist or the researcher conducting a field study. Their use is relatively straightforward and is often facilitated by employing a standard layout for each type of observation to be made. Frequently appropriate blanks can be Xeroxed to be filled in and filed in a binder as required.

Interview notes and similar materials are rather more difficult to structure because it is hard to predetermine the course of an interview. Nevertheless there will in most cases be an interview schedule listing the topics to be covered and this may well serve as the basis of a data gathering instrument with half a page, say, being allocated to each subject heading. With a little experience it is usually possible for the researcher to generate his own 'shorthand' for recording thus enabling him to come nearer to a verbatim record. In view of the high information content of pictorial data it makes obvious sense to record data in that form, where possible.

Questionnaires provide a more structured approach to gathering data of this type. Where closed questions, that is, those which provide for only a limited list of responses are used, subsequent transcription is particularly easy. It pays to design them from the outset with computer processing in mind if it is intended that they should be analysed by computer eventually. In practice the novice researcher is well advised to consult with those who will be responsible for entering data from his questionnaire into the computer.

Tape recorders are generally acceptable in most interviewing situations subject perhaps, to certain parts of the interview being 'off the record'. Cassette recorders are sufficiently portable for two to be used, preferably with tapes of different playing time to allow for continuity during changeovers and a measure of backup. It may well be worth carrying both 'narrow' and 'wide angle' microphones so that the most appropriate type can be selected.

One aspect of tape recording which is frequently overlooked by student researchers is the cost of transcription which may amount to several hundreds of pounds if many interviews are involved.

For these reasons and to cope with the situations where they are not acceptable the student still needs other methods of recording. Though the act of taking notes can be useful in pacing an interview, the ideal method is one that the student can carry out while still looking at the interviewee. At a minimum this will usually require some sort of shorthand or code with the ideal being the ability to recall every detail of the interview (remembering that non-verbal behaviour is often more important) an hour afterwards. Certainly the typical student will usually find it useful to write notes on the interview as soon as possible after it has taken place.

Lightweight video cameras are straightforward to use and are becoming increasingly available. The largest barrier to their wider employment now that domestic video tape recorders are becoming fairly common is the difficulty of transcribing some part of the enormous amount of data contained in a video tape into a form suitable for analysis.

Chart recorders are still widely used in conjunction with many types of measuring equipment, for example, temperature recording. Since they lend themselves to online connection to the computer it seems likely that they will eventually be replaced by datalogging equipment, (that is equipment which records measurements that can be fed directly into a computer analysis). It should be remembered though that chart records of, say, seismograph readings from past earthquakes may well continue to be important data sources.

Another method is one that enables the data to be transmitted directly to a computer file with the obvious attractions noted earlier. The first group of such methods are those that were developed for commercial purposes, for example, the tally roll printouts produced by the older type of cash register. Perhaps the most neglected one from the point of view of student research is the mark sense reader capable of recording the presence or absence of a pencil tick in a box in a specified position on a sheet of paper. These are widely used in the US for, amongst other purposes, providing automatic marking of multiple choice examinations.

One commercial data recording method that is beginning to find application in research is direct encoding onto cassette tape. Such recorders were originally developed for stock control in supermarkets where the item code number and a count of the number actually on the shelves were entered on to the tape along, perhaps, with the time at which the data were entered. Similar devices are now being used in many types of observation of human behaviour to record the type of behaviour, the time of its onset and the time of its completion (cf. Sawin *et al.*, 1977).

Finally for the scientist or engineer there are the 'dataloggers' referred to above. Their use is widespread and growing as microcomputers are increasingly used for this purpose. However the user of such facilities may be faced with a somewhat unexpected transcription problem, if, as is often the case, he wishes to carry out his analysis on a different type of computer from that on which his data were originally input. The ease with which data can be transferred from one machine to another varies markedly depending on the computers involved. The researcher is accordingly well advised to explore how easy the transfer will be before carrying out his experiments so that if necessary he can use a different computer for datalogging or for analysis.

b) Transcription Methods

The standard method of transcribing data for computer input is still to write out the numbers on to punching documents. The process of verification by duplication has already been described and for data sets larger than a few dozen numbers it is advisable to get data verified in this way if possible. Most educational institutions are not however able to afford this process and it is only the researcher who has access to private funds who is likely to be able to pay for it. The alternative is to employ a variety of checks already discussed in the context of validation. A further useful device is to demand that the data be input in a rigid format. For example, if our numbers are up to 4 digits long it is possible to fit sixteen of them on to the usual 80 character input line leaving a space between each. Provided that where necessary leading zeros are supplied so that 32 is typed as 0032, the fifth, tenth, and fifteenth character positions and so forth should be blank. This can be verified on input, and any input lines that fail the test are then corrected. Such a test detects, for example, accidental double punching, for example, 00322 for 0032. It will not however detect the other common form of transcription error, namely, transposition, for example, 0023 for 0032 which the student researcher will still have to guard against.

Provided any necessary agreement has been secured in advance there should be no trouble in getting data entered into the computer directly from well designed questionnaires or similar documents as long as these have been correctly completed.

Pictorial information can be reduced to numbers in at least two different ways. Firstly graphs and curves can be converted to a corresponding set of horizontal and vertical co-ordinates using a digitiser. Line information can similarly be converted to numbers by using a light pen.

Another type of device is the densitometer that measures the blackness of individual points in a picture and converts them to a numerical value. There are also many circumstances in which it is required to analyse textual data. An obvious example is in the production of concordances and another is the content analysis of a set of interviews where it is required to find all instances where two or more ideas or variables appear together. Word processing facilities which are extremely useful for such purposes, will be discussed further in Chapter 8.

PREPARING FOR DATA GATHERING

Though in certain parts of the social sciences, in particular, the view is sometimes expressed that all data are inevitably partly subjective, we do not feel that such a view is generally helpful to the student researcher whose aim is to complete his research successfully in a reasonable time. Accordingly we would see the demonstration that the researcher has gathered his data in a fashion that could be repeated by himself or others and lead (allowing for measurement error) to the same results as a matter of practical as well as philosophical importance. Usually however this is not a trivial matter. Measuring instruments must be calibrated and the researcher must become sufficiently familiar with the techniques he is using to be able to obtain satisfactory results. Even an apparently simple task such as the accurate determination of the relative proportions of salt and sand in a mixture can require a lot of practice before it can be carried out successfully. In more complex situations such as the observation of the interactions of two different groups within a factory the researcher may well find that his perception of what say constitutes, aggressive behaviour, changes as he becomes more familiar with the context. In both cases it is clearly important that the researcher allows enough time to 'calibrate' himself as well as any equipment he may need, and this has obvious implications for planning the research project as discussed in Chapter 3.

ORGANISING THE DATA

Whichever of the above methods is used to gather data it will normally be necessary to maintain an extensive set of supplementary notes on the sources of the data, the conditions under which they were gathered, their relationships to other sets of data, and so on. These need to be stored in such a way as to offer some reasonable prospect of retrieval when required. Where much information is involved it is best to store the notes in folders which are then preferably stored in a filing cabinet. Deciding on a list of subject headings under which to file is similar to generating a thesaurus for literature surveying as discussed in Chapter 4. In many cases it will be obvious that notes could profitably be filed under more than one heading. Where they are brief this is perhaps most easily accommodated by producing several Xerox copies. Where the material is more bulky cross references of the form, 'Note on possible method of assessing the innovativeness of individual engineers, 23.10.81, see file on Measuring characteristics of individual engineers' can be filed under the relevant subjects.

Such concerns are perhaps particularly relevant where data are subject to computer analysis. It is often possible to find students repeating a computer run because insufficient information was kept about the original one for its results to be located. Nevertheless this is an illustration of a far more general point. Effective management of data gathering, requires that thought be given to the organisation of the data early in this phase of the project before any retrospective attempt to impose some system and order upon them becomes infeasible. As in many other situations the important thing is to have a workable rather than a perfect system.

A very readable account of the latest methods of organising and retrieving data has been written by Stibic (1980). Students whose projects are planned to last for two or three years should obtain considerable benefit by following up this reference.

COLLECTING PRIMARY DATA

In order to discuss the practical aspects of the collection of primary data it is necessary to break them down into a number of categories namely: laboratory measurements; field observation; archives/collections; questionnaires, and interviews. Whilst it cannot be pretended that this list is exhaustive there are important differences between the various sources listed. The brief comments are designed to highlight aspects which are pertinent to the planning and successful execution of this phase of student research.

Laboratory Measurement

Laboratory measurements typically offer the researcher the greatest control over his data gathering activities and therefore lend themselves to careful planning. The most important considerations are usually to design the apparatus or experiment to collect and record the necessary data as efficiently as possible, to construct it and to ensure it is working correctly. This can take a great deal of time.

Efficient design is primarily a matter of considering the way in which the data will be used in analysis. To verify that gravity attracts objects towards the earth rather than repelling them needs only very simple apparatus and few observations. To determine the law governing that attraction however requires much better equipment and a lot more measurements. Beyond that it is worth remembering that since extreme measurements always provide a better test of theories there is much to be said for attempting to design apparatus to cope with a wider range of measurements than it is believed will be needed.

Building a test rig or organising an experimental situation can often be speeded up by formal methods of planning of the type described in Chapter 3. Ensuring that the experiment is functioning as intended and that data are being properly recorded is often harder to plan. The researcher can at least though give proper consideration to the things that might be wrong with his data and ways in which they could be detected at an early stage, for example, by using a duplicate measuring device from time to time to provide a spot check on his main instrument.

Though it is obviously important to detect erroneous data and situations where the experiment is not functioning as planned, the opposite problem also exists of being too willing to abandon data because they are 'not right' or because something must have been wrong with the experiment when they were collected. This can lead to important behaviour being rejected in the name of consistency. All experimenters recognise that there are situations under which data must be rejected for these reasons. Against this, scientific data are often suspiciously tidy with much less error than might have been expected on a statistical basis.

Field Observation

Many types of research, for example, geophysical and ecological, make heavy use of field observation. Where possible it is better to use simple, familiar measuring equipment capable of operating reliably under field conditions for carrying out measurements in the field.

Field observations of human behaviour are of so many different types that it is hardly possible to do more than state some of their major advantages and disadvantages. For a comprehensive discussion of such topics with particular reference to the social sciences the reader is recommended to consult the book by Webb et al. (1966).

Where the observations cannot be carried out without the knowledge of the subjects as say in anthropological data gathering the researcher may well cause unrepresentative behaviour repertoires to be displayed in his presence. For the student interested in this type of observation it is worthwhile consulting the obvious sources of expertise, namely, the cultural anthropologists or sociologists interested in deviant groups. Relevant material can be found for example in Naroll (1962), which also discusses the problem raised earlier of how the researcher's perceptions and therefore the basis of data collection can change as the field observations progress and ways in which it can be overcome. The ideas of Glaser and Strauss (1967) and in particular their emphasis on continual restatement of the theory on which data gathering is based are also of considerable interest in this context.

Field observation need not always be completely passive. Substantial experimental manipulation may be possible even though the complete control of the laboratory situation is not possible.

Situations of this type can often lend themselves to analysis by the statistical experimental design model discussed in Chapter 5. Interpretation of the results is not usually however anywhere near as simple as in the laboratory situation and generalisability is often more difficult to assess because of doubts about how typical the field situation is.

Archival Data

Many subjects make extensive use of data available in some type of archive or collection. In many countries locally maintained records and the minutes of learned societies are important data sources for the historian. The archaeologist is likely to make extensive use of museum collections of artefacts. The accurate astronomical records kept by certain ancient civilisations are of importance in some branches of astronomy and so on.

Less well recognised is the existence of private archives or caches of data (Glaser and Strauss, 1967). Many private collections of paintings, for example, are not publicised for insurance reasons. On the other hand there is a mass of material available to the researcher, and arising from records of normal day-to-day business for which this problem does not exist. If the student can discover the existence of such a collection and obtain access to it then the prospects of producing interesting research findings are well above average.

For recognised collections it is often possible to obtain access for the purpose of *bona fide* research. The problems for the researcher interested in archives of this sort are to obtain sufficient resources to visit them (since there is little prospect of borrowing the material) and then to find some satisfactory way of recording (since the data involved are rarely intrinsically easy to record and there may well be limitations on say the photographing of old documents). Some archives of this kind are available as facsimiles, for example, photographs of drawings or microfiches of company accounts and for these it should usually be possible to find sufficient money to pay for copies of major items of interest. Academic bodies have traditionally looked favourably on the provision of travel grants and scholarships specifically for visiting archives and similarly there may be some possibility of obtaining funds from the sponsor of the student's research.

A number of methods of finding out about private collections have been suggested by Glaser and Strauss (1967) but since they are rarely compiled for research purposes, obtaining access can be difficult. As stated earlier the student will often obtain access more easily if a request is made on his behalf by someone of suitable academic distinction. Furthermore it is probably most common for access to non-government material if granted, to be restricted to a few individuals at most. In broad terms, then, it is rarely worth trying to gain access to private material on which other researchers are already working.

Gathering Data by Questionnaires

Questionnaires have over the past century, become a common method of gathering information. Their design is a large subject that will not be attempted here, and the reader is advised to consult a specialist text, for example, Moser and Kalton, 1971; Berdie and Anderson, 1974. The concern here is with some of the practical problems that occur in using questionnaires. Since the administration of questionnaires during an interview shares many of the problems of interviewing, we shall concentrate first on the use of questionnaires for postal surveys.

Postal surveys are a favoured way of seeking to acquire data from a large number of respondents. Inevitably the quality of the data gathered is more superficial than that which can be collected during an interview so the tendency is usually for the study to be a large one. This in turn means that there will be large quantities of data to process. In almost all cases this favours the use of a computer, the implications of which have already been discussed.

The biggest problem with the postal questionnaire is that it is only somewhat tenuously a primary data gathering method. The investigator may have no direct contact with his respondents who may interpret his questions very differently from his intention. A pilot survey, however modest, is therefore essential. It need not observe the strict procedures necessary later with regard to sample selection providing it indicates realistically how the questions will be interpreted. Another less used procedure principally employed in crosscultural studies is that of back translation. The questionnaire is translated from, say English to Arabic by one person and then from Arabic to English by another and the resulting version compared with the original (Warwick and Osherson, 1973).

In a postal survey it would usually be considered unwise to have a questionnaire requiring more than about fifteen minutes to fill in or covering more than say ten pages. Too long a questionnaire is likely to markedly reduce the percentage of responses and a low response rate always raises questions of bias. As outlined in the last chapter this problem can to some extent be overcome by including additional questions that enable the researcher to check whether the returns are typical of the sampled population but this has the disadvantage of increasing the length of the questionnaire. Accordingly other steps will often need to be taken too. In many situations, for example, measuring the demand for molybdenum, a small number of responding companies account for the bulk of the behaviour of interest and since they are likely to be large and efficient there may well be definite advantages in eschewing the traditional random sample in favour of 100 per cent coverage of this fairly small group. Where random samples are deemed necessary it may be possible to administer the questionnaire by telephone. Certainly a telephone call to enlist the co-operation of potential respondents often handsomely increases the response rate. The sponsorship of a prestigious body, such as a professional association can also improve response considerably. In most circumstances it is usually necessary anyway to send a suitably worded follow-up letter to non-respondents. Since response rates can vary from under 5 per cent to 80 per cent or so depending on the above factors it clearly behoves the researcher to consider these points. If this is not done he may end up with a small number of possibly biased returns that are insufficient for the purposes of his analysis and he will also be in no position to draw up a realistic budget for the resources required during this part of his study.

Interviews

Most social scientists would see the interview as providing higher quality information that is freer from bias than many other methods available to them. Indeed in a new field a programme of interviews may be the only way of obtaining a realistic picture of the way people view it. Such rich potential does of course imply a need for planning and training, if the student is to make the most of the interview programme he has organised. Many factors are relevant here from basic points like the need to be punctual through to considerably more complex topics such as how to probe a particular subject in a non-directive way. A number of texts deal with these points at length, for example, Gorden (1975), and the reader is referred to these for further details.

The major data gathering problems in interviewing are to find adequate ways of recording all the data given. These in turn relate to the degree to which the interviewer wishes to structure the interview and in fact is permitted to do so (since the research student's control over an interview with, for example, a managing director is somewhat limited). An interview can in fact, be just a means of getting a lengthy and complex questionnaire filled in. Usually, however, the student will wish to supplement this by open-ended discussion and a more common model is for the interviewer to define a schedule of topics to be covered and to explore them in whatever order appears natural in the course of the discussion. This situation is obviously more difficult to handle. At a very minimum two things are needed: some way of discreetly keeping a check that all topics have been covered and an initial icebreaking question that is almost guaranteed to evoke a response from the interviewee. This problem is obviously exacerbated by the fact that under most circumstances interviews should probably not take much over an hour and indeed the researcher may have far less time at his disposal if the subject is one that is of little interest to the interviewee.

Generally it is not desirable to schedule more than two or three interviews a day which implies that the typical student researcher cannot afford a very extensive programme for reasons of both time and money. Thought also needs to be devoted as to how they are to be analysed in the final research report, otherwise the researcher runs the risk of having a wealth of data from a set of individually valuable interviews that collectively are very difficult to generalise from and which he cannot afford to repeat. The preparation of a realistic interview schedule in advance of the first interview is clearly a wise step towards meeting this aim.

Further uses for Primary Data

Frequently primary data gathered for one purpose turn out to be of great value for totally different purposes at a later date. It is by no means unknown for a researcher to return to his data years after his immediate objective of writing a thesis has been achieved. And, like bibliographies, they may represent a tradeable commodity that will facilitate access to other researchers' data. It follows then that where possible primary data should be carefully filed away along with sufficient details to enable them to be used by someone else. Similarly where some part of them has been transcribed on to the computer those data should be put on to magnetic tape so that they are available for future use.

SECONDARY DATA SOURCES

By secondary data is meant data collected by others and published in some form that is fairly readily accessible. Thus in these terms company accounts that are published by law are secondary data. In general the research student will not know much about the hidden assumptions, corrections or distortions that go into the production of a particular set of secondary data unless he takes the trouble to find out what these were.

Such data tend to have the beguiling look of the printed page about them and may thus appear far removed from the messy imperfections and inconsistencies that the researcher may know to exist in his primary data. For the social scientist it is salutary to read Morgernstern's (1963) compendious review of the myriad ways in which economic and social data can involve error and bias. Whatever the researcher's interest it is always wise to ascertain the basis on which measurements are compiled since otherwise different sets taken under different conditions or using different methods may well not be comparable. In addition many data involve substantial measurement error and it may well be important in the analysis to be aware of this.

On the other side of the coin secondary data have considerable attractions for the research student particularly in the social sciences and especially if he is engaged in a short research project. They are usually more quickly available than primary data and much less organisation is required to obtain them. Furthermore they exist in considerable quantities and may contain information that is fairly easy for a government agency with legal backing to collect that would be very difficult for the lone researcher.

Figure 6.2 lists a number of important sources and types of secondary data, and these are reviewed briefly paying attention to some of the main

Source	Type of data
Technical publications (Manuals / handbooks / data sheets / standards)	— Physical / chemical constants Technical performance specifications
Books and journals	— 'Workhorse data' More esoteric quantitative data of all kinds Non quantitative data
Official publications (e.g. Central and Local Government)	— Economic / social data
Trade association data	— Technical or economic data
Private data services	— Economic / product data
Computer databases	— All types of quantitative data

Figure 6.2   Some sources and types of secondary data

advantages and problems of each source and referring the reader where desirable to more specialist sources for discussions of particular types.

Technical Publications

A host of data from physical and chemical constants to performance data for particular items of equipment are to be found in handbooks and manuals. Publications of this type are familiar names to workers in a particular field, for example, *Spon's Architects' and Builders' Price Book*. Similar information may be published by equipment manufacturers in the form of detailed performance specifications or by trade associations or bodies such as the British Standard Institution. Most data of this sort are relatively easily accessible. The basic techniques of literature searching will usually reveal what are available in an academic library.

Books and Journals

For many researchers books and journals are likely to be the major source of data. Furthermore, they are by far the most important source of what has been called textual data.

One major use of books and journals is in providing certain standard sets of 'workhorse data' that are used by all investigators in a field as test beds for new methods and techniques so that their performance can be compared with well established ones. Very often they will be found in the literature of a subject, for example, the various time series, such as IBM common stock price and sales of airline seats, used to compare different computer methods of forecasting (Box and Jenkins, 1976).

The data presented in a book or paper have typically received more processing and may therefore be subject to more qualifications than other types of secondary data. Indeed they frequently are based on refinements and reworking of existing secondary data though this may not be readily apparent.

On the whole unless the research project is short or the data are only of peripheral interest the use of books as sources of other than 'workhorse data' is perhaps best restricted to those which focus on the assumptions and processes by which the data were generated or to those providing expensive or esoteric data not readily available elsewhere.

Official Publications

The volume and diversity of government publications has already been remarked on in Chapter 4. In advanced economies these are a major source of social and economic data of all kinds as well as design and performance specifications for many fields of engineering, and so forth. For a comprehensive account of British Government publications the reader is advised to consult *'British Official Publications'* (Pemberton, 1973).

The most frequently useful official data are probably the various statistics compiled by government departments. By way of example more detailed accounts of UK Government statistics on population and related matters can be found in Pickett (1974) and in *'Facts in Focus'*, CSO/Penguin Books (1978) or the Open University Course Unit D291 (1975).

Though discovering what official sources are available is usually relatively straightforward, guidance as to how to make effective use of the information is in our experience more difficult to come by. Frequently the researcher needs to carry out further manipulations of the data listed, perhaps by comparing data in one source with those in another. Such are the diversity of uses of government statistics that even the experienced social science researcher is only likely to know a few of the sources well. The student researcher can probably learn much about how to exploit such data from talks and seminars given by those who make regular use of them, that is, market researchers, economists, educational sociologists and so forth.

There are many other public bodies that publish statistics of importance to the researcher. In the UK, for instance, organisations such as the National Economic Development Office publish much material of a statistical nature and the reports of the nationalised industries go far beyond the provision of statutory accounting data in describing their operations.

The official statistics of other countries are another useful source for the researcher as are those of international bodies such as OECD and UNESCO, all of which can provide important data for comparative purposes. Many of these find their way in the *'United Nations Statistical Yearbook'*.

Lists of the official statistics of various countries can be found, for example, in Harvey (1973) which gives a guide to American (including Central and South America) statistics, principally aimed at the market researcher. A much more comprehensive list of European sources can be found in Harvey (1976).

Data of this type come in the category of those that the researcher could not possibly collect for himself. Rather he must make the best use of what exists and from the point of view of the research report that means critically appraising the data available to him assessing their defects and correcting or allowing for them as best he can.

There are many types of research that require historical data. Numerous official statistics have been collected in the past in connection with a decennial census or a particular survey. Certain data series, such as wheat prices, extend back over a substantial period. Two useful guides to UK historical data series are Mitchell and Deane (1962) and Mitchell and Jones (1971). A similar guide to European series also exists (Mitchell, 1975).

Trade Association Data

Trade associations and similar bodies can be an excellent source of both technical and economic data about the operations of their members. For obvious reasons the economic data they publish are more detailed than those available through official statistics. Information on UK trade associations can be found in the *Directory of British Associations* and the availability of data can be checked with the relevant association.

Private Data Services

Data that are of interest to the researcher can often be of considerable use to researchers in general particularly those working in the private sector in market research, investment analysis, and so on. Data of this type are accordingly a commercial proposition and there are many different services available. Sometimes access to them is free as with trade catalogues and permanent exhibitions. More usually they cost money. Many are available on a subscription basis, for example, the Extel Service giving details of the accounts of companies listed on UK Stock Exchanges, and are to be found in larger public libraries as well as academic libraries. Some appear regularly – often annually – for example, guides to UK markets. Other data are produced only on a one-off basis and tend to be far more expensive, for example, the multi-client studies produced by certain organisations giving data on various products and markets that typically are intended to be sold only to a few dozen organisations. Often those services that provide information not readily accessible to the academic researcher, for example, details of executive remuneration for different types of post in different countries, are likely to be most useful and for that reason expensive, so their use has to be budgeted for at the planning stage.

Computer Databases

A source of secondary data that is rapidly growing in importance is the computer database. In the UK many Central Statistical Office Series are now available on computer bureaux, as are accounting data for listed public companies. The increasing importance of bibliographic databases and the possibility of using them as a data source has been noted in Chapter 4. Similar remarks apply to the databases for products and services now available in a variety of fields. International bodies also maintain important databases, for example, the United Nations database on trade flows. Further information on available databases can be found, for example, in the *EUSIDIC Directory* (Tomberg, 1978). Many have been developed directly by universities and other institutions for research purposes, and will often be available to researchers from elsewhere.

Where they exist databases are a very valuable form of secondary data. They usually contain far more observations than the individual student could collect and the basis on which the data have been gathered and the adjustments made are usually explicit. Most importantly they are ideally suited to computer analysis and make it quite feasible for the individual student to contemplate types of analysis and research topics that would have been considered hopelessly ambitious even ten years ago.

On the whole the student researcher needs free access to the data so that he can experiment with different ways of processing them. This usually means copying the database on magnetic tape and transferring the details on to his own computer system. This transfer cannot always be effected directly but may for technical computing reasons require that the data first be transferred to some intermediate computer and thence to the system used by the researcher. This can usually be organised and carried out in a few weeks provided that, where necessary, tapes are sent airmail. At the minimum, the cost of transfer of a very large database may only be that of the tape, the postage and a small amount of computer time, for example, when the database owner is another university (particularly a US one) or some public body. Where the system is a commercial one the cost may be several hundred pounds (if the owner is willing to make a copy available) because payment is expected for the data themselves. Additionally there are almost always restrictions on the use the researcher may make of the information, for example, it is unlikely he will be allowed to sell it to others. Whatever the source it is probable that he will need to budget for further copies of the database at regular intervals so that he can keep his version up to date.

Unless he is familiar with the procedures involved we would strongly advise the research student who wishes to obtain a copy of a database to leave the details of the transfer to the computer department of his own institution since they will be in a better position to judge how to do it easily and to liaise with the staff of the computer centre on which the database is maintained. Once he has acquired a copy of the data base however we would urge the student to acquire the skills needed to enable him to carry out his own analyses. At worst this is unlikely to involve him in little more than learning how to handle files in some common computer language such as FORTRAN. At best he may find that his installation possesses a file interrogation package that makes the process very straightforward. In either case he will have acquired a skill that might well benefit him in his subsequent career.

Obviously conversion of the database to a usable form and the acquisition of the necessary computing skills both require time, and the former may involve expense if it is not carried out by the student himself. Prospective use of a database has, therefore, important implications for the planning of the research.

SUMMARY

DATA MAY BE DISTINGUISHED AS: Primary data – data gathered by the researcher and secondary data – data gathered by others.

DATA MUST BE: located
assessed
collected and checked
recorded in a form suitable for
subsequent analysis.

MEASUREMENT ERROR: affects much data and must be reduced to an acceptable level, possibly by increasing the sample size.

DATA GATHERING: is a demanding activity when primary data are involved and time should be allocated for training in collection. Secondary data are usually easier to collect and use although the assumptions on which this type of data are based may be unclear.

DATA ORGANISATION: thought should be given to how best to organise the data and associated notes on them to avoid wasted effort through reduplication of analyses, etc.

DATA RECORDING: usually involves the two processes of capture and transcription. Where possible means of error checking should be employed at both of these stages.

COMPUTER DATABASES: incorporating statistical series and the like are increasingly becoming available for the researcher.

PART C:

PRODUCING THE
RESEARCH RESULTS

7

Executing the Research

Whatever the level of the research students should resist the temptation to proceed with its execution until an acceptable plan has been formulated. It would be a mistake, however, to assume that when this has been achieved the research will proceed towards its conclusion with as much certainty as the construction of a bridge. Even the smaller project which is planned to be completed within a few months may encounter unexpected obstacles.

This chapter has three main objectives:

1. to identify problems which with hindsight could have been avoided and to suggest anticipatory action which should be adopted;
2. to suggest ways of coping with unavoidable or unexpected problems which may arise;
3. to make positive suggestions which will facilitate research progress.

151

AVOIDABLE PROBLEMS

In large part these should be highlighted by the systematic planning process described in Chapter 3. There are, nevertheless, three aspects which should continue to receive attention throughout the course of the study:

a) overcommitment;
b) failure to make use of the research plan;
c) adequacy of supervision.

It is appreciated that supervisors may be appointed at different stages of the research according to the approach used by the particular institution. Thus the link may be established prior to topic selection, between that and the research proposal, or after the proposal. Part-time students may not be accepted in some cases until they have presented a carefully argued research proposal. As, however, most supervision will be undertaken during the execution of the research the practice is discussed at greatest length in this chapter.

Overcommitment

Reference was made in Chapter 1 to a survey of students which was designed to assess why completion rates were not as good as they might have been. Several activities were identified as competing for available time and certain of these were felt, on balance, to affect progress adversely.

It is not suggested that once students embark upon a research project they should turn their backs on all other types of activity; there should be scope for both leisure and academic related pursuits. This book is not concerned with the former which must remain the responsibility of the student but with those opportunities which present themselves to full-time research students and which may be perceived as potential contributors to self-development in a career sense or simply as a means of generating much needed income. It is appreciated that our comments will relate more to those undertaking longer periods of study.

A difficult decision for some research degree students to take is the extent to which they accept tutorial or demonstrating work offered to them.[1] Many such students have inclinations to pursue a career in education and apart from the financial benefits see the experience as being of much potential value. It is important that before accepting a teaching commitment the student should investigate the total demand which it will make on his time. A one hour tutorial may involve three hours preparation and two hours marking. Since many research students would see fifty hours of actual work a week as being realistic, ten hours commitment arising from a regular teaching assignment would be a substantial proportion of this total. Certainly time in excess of this could have a major adverse effect on the rate of progress of the study itself. It is, however, by no means rare for a student to acquire a reputation during the course of his research and as a result to be invited to give one-off lectures. In moderation the acceptance of invitations of this nature are to be encouraged, not least so that advantage can be taken of constructive criticism when he comes to writing his thesis.

The student who anticipates that he will from time to time present the findings of his work in a more or less formal setting would do well to read the booklet 'Talking about your research' (Dixon and Hills, 1981). In addition to advice on visual aids and communicating with an audience the booklet includes a number of useful references on script preparation.

The preparation of papers on topics arising from, or very closely related to, the research has much to commend it. In addition to gaining valuable experience of the writing process itself the acceptance of articles for publication is probably the main way in which academic reputations are established. Additionally a measure of substance is added to research theses if the student can reference his own work which has been published in journals of repute. It would therefore be quite reasonable for a student to think in terms of submitting articles for publication at a rate of about one per year of full-time study.

The opportunity for consultancy does not come the way of more than a small fraction of students. Such offers are usually tempting to the impecunious student and may even add considerably to his research, but their acceptance may jeopardise the completion of his work. Perhaps the only advice that can be given is that if the student is not prepared to contemplate being unable to finish his thesis on time he should only undertake consultancy if by careful and realistic planning he estimates that the additional work can be accommodated.

The survey referred to above listed 'Other outside work'. This will be assumed here to include all extra-research activities not so far consi-

1. In the UK both the SSRC and the SERC encourage graduate student to undertake teaching providing that not more than six hours a week (including preparation) is spent on this activity. Also permitted is a small amount of other paid work providing that the supervisor's approval is obtained.

dered but which do not qualify as leisure in the usually accepted sense of that word. A good deal depends on the extent to which the student is involved in any of the activities already referred to (teaching, writing papers, and consultancy). If he is not greatly involved he could well benefit from doing something to counterbalance research which may be very demanding and at times tedious. The work content of taught degree courses is fairly well defined, research on the other hand can be virtually unbounded. The research student should not be guilt-ridden if, he takes time off to run a society, edit a student's paper, or organise a wine tasting.

In practice the most important determinant of the amount of the outside activity in which the research student can safely engage is his ability to organise his own time effectively. There are students who manage a very substantial part-time commitment to research whilst at the same time occupying very senior positions in large organisations. Equally full-time research students are known who successfully combine a very active role in research with a substantial part-time commitment to a company as an executive or as a director. Conversely many research students, particularly younger ones, find considerable difficulty in organising their own time effectively enough to carry on the single task of research.

A wise student will appreciate that the assumption that during a two or three year study major diversions can be absorbed without prejudicing successful completion is a dangerous one. It is vital that he should never let his research get out of control. It is, therefore, strongly recommended that he should maintain schedule charts, update these at least once every two weeks, and avoid any binding commitment if there is a high probability that as a result the study will be unacceptably extended.

Failure to make use of the Research Plan

In Chapter 3 the importance of fixing 'milestones' in the project was discussed, and in particular their use for ensuring that progress is maintained. Experience suggests that many students do not place sufficient weight on meeting the deadlines they identify, or on redefining and replanning the research if for some reason a milestone is missed by any considerable length of time. This is particularly so at the doctoral level where there are few natural markers of the passage of time. The end result can be that each stage takes longer than planned and, eventually, what once seemed a leisurely schedule now seems hopelessly optimistic given the time remaining.

A further and often more serious variant of this problem is to refuse to admit that a serious snag has been encountered. Surprisingly often, research students find that a particular stage in the research is more difficult than was envisaged but are unwilling to admit to themselves that the problem is a major one. Instead they begin to look a day or two ahead to the time when the bug will certainly have been removed from the computer program or their apparatus will finally begin to work, and eventually many months can be wasted in a welter of misplaced optimism.

Such situations can be avoided if the student realises he has a problem and seeks advice about it. If he continually reviews his progress against a plan it is unlikely that he will seriously deceive himself whereas if he does not he will almost certainly find it far more difficult to seek help given the embarrassingly long time it took him to see the need.

Adequacy of Supervision

Students undertaking even short research projects have a right to expect to receive advice, supervision, or direction. Literal interpretation suggests that the degree of control exercised over the student increases from an advisor, through a supervisor, to a director. All of the latter categories are encountered but the most common in British higher degree research is the supervisor. The word 'supervision' is a fairly accurate reflection of the context in which research is most appropriately conducted, containing elements of both 'advice' when requested and 'direction' when deemed apposite by the supervisor. To some extent attitudes of supervisors are affected by the fact that demands made upon them differ from those which arise in traditional teaching situations. They may feel a lack of competence in research methodology and in coping with problems which arise in areas with which they are unfamiliar. More fundamental is the degree of obligation which the supervisor carries for the successful completion of a research study. In many courses two conditions need to be met. The first is that the report or dissertation must be handed in by a particular date, the second requires that minimum standards should be satisfied. Postgraduate degrees are often based wholly or in part on dissertations or theses for which the submission date is flexible within what might be quite an extended period. Although degree awarding institutions define the latest date of normal submission, extensions are usually granted if the student can provide evidence that he is continuing to make some progress. On the assumption that few students can obtain finance for full-time study for more than two or three years this points to the research being completed part-time. In these circumstances (even though the student may be paying substantial fees) supervision can become lax and solely reactive. This is, to an extent, understandable as staff members move to new interests and new appointments. If, therefore, a student is taking an inordinate time to complete his project he must expect the initiative for supervision to be largely his responsibility (although this does not absolve the supervisor entirely from action as long as the student continues to be formally registered).

The position of the student registered for a part-time research degree is rather different from that of the full-time student. Very often his research will be related to his work in which case he may expect reasonable support from his organisation. In fact some statement to this effect from his employer will often be required by the institution with which he is registered along with formal evidence that adequate supervision will be available. In many cases an industrial supervisor may be appointed or, if the candidate is located overseas an additional academic supervisor may need to be found locally.

Some academics prefer to supervise part-time research degrees on the grounds that only the highly motivated student will embark on one and that they frequently have access to much richer data sources, such as confidential company records, that are not usually available to the full-time student. The part-time student, moreover, is often more willing to organise the details of the supervisor/student relationship than many full-time students. Indeed, given that his research must be fitted in around the requirements of a job, it is normally best if he undertakes this responsibility. Meetings and discussions with his supervisor should, desirably, take place at least quarterly and, in many cases, these will be supplemented by submission of written material particularly in the writing up stage. Provided he does this, and manages to stick to his original plans the part-time researcher's chances of success are good, particularly if he is able to attend courses or better still register for an extended period (say 6 months to a year) full-time once he and his supervisors are satisfied that he can complete successfully.

UNAVOIDABLE OR UNEXPECTED PROBLEMS

In addition to those things which the student should plan to avoid he must also recognise that his research can be threatened by many other factors. It is suggested that the student should be aware of these possibilities but should not 'over-plan' to cover every conceivable contingency which may occur. These problems are described as being unavoidable or unexpected. Figure 7.1 groups this type of problem.

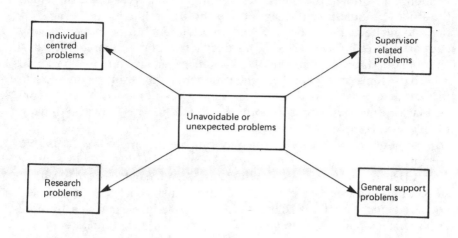

Figure 7.1   Types of unavoidable or unexpected problems

Individual Centred Problems

There are a number of ways in which research progress may be affected by what may be termed 'personal' factors:

a) illness;
b) loss of motivation;
c) occurrence of other opportunities;
d) need to search for a job.

Illness affecting the student or his close relatives is always a possibility. It is likely to have an adversely non-linear effect as the duration of illness increases. Ten per cent of available time is probably the maximum which the student can accommodate and supervisors or examiners should be made aware if five per cent of research time is likely to be affected by illness.

Institutions and grant awarding bodies are sympathetic towards students who suffer illness and it is much to be preferred that such incidence is notified. If the illness is of long duration the decision which the student should take is clear cut. He should seek to have his registration suspended and, if he is a full-time student, to have part of any support he receives deferred. The decision becomes more difficult if shorter periods of illness are involved when there may be an inclination to absorb the time lost and at the same time retain any grant payment. The proportion of the planned period remaining will obviously be an important factor. If the student is in doubt he should incline towards delaying his planned completion date.

Without self-motivation research can be extremely laborious. No student can maintain the same pitch of enthusiasm throughout a study particularly if it is of several years duration. A range of factors may lead to a loss of motivation. These include tedium, frustration, lack of progress and a reduction in interest. There is little need to give examples, of more importance is how problems of this type may be overcome.

The first recommendation is that they should be discussed informally with someone else; preferably the supervisor in the first instance, but also with students who have experienced and overcome similar difficulties. If informal discussions do not bring about the desired outcome then a second possibility is that the student should suggest to his supervisor that an *ad hoc* committee should be set up to review progress. Some institutions use this practice routinely and it is usually found to be very effective. Two or three faculty members (one of whom may have no experience in the field of research) are often able to generate suggestions which indicate how problems may be resolved or which stimulate the student's interest in his topic.

A third possibility which may help in overcoming tedium, in particular during the early stages of research, is to leave aside the task in hand and switch to another. Figure 3.3, the schedule control chart, shows that several parallel activities may have been identified. Unless the activity creating the problem is 'critical' the student can probably find something completely different to pursue and, importantly, will be able to assess how long a task may be deferred before it becomes critical. An example of an activity which can be both motivating and rewarding is the writing of a paper on a distinct phase of the work which has been completed. Even though the paper may be a general one reviewing the current situation in the area, or a descriptive account of the response to a survey, acceptance for publication can be a spur to renewed effort besides having other obvious advantages.

The ability to 'stand back' particularly during the longer studies, and view tedium and frustration as being inevitable from time to time should go some way to overcoming motivational problems. To this end the use of some type of wall chart as described in Chapter 3 will emphasise progress which has been made.

If having tried all means of self-motivation without effect the student should not lose sight of the responsibility borne by the supervisor. On first being acquainted with the difficulties being experienced the supervisor will no doubt have made a number of suggestions for the student to follow up. As the student is unable on his own to resolve his difficulties the supervisor should play a much more active role; but this is only possible if he is kept fully informed.

Those students for whom their research is the whole basis of their degree are often confronted with another type of problem; that arising from offers of employment. Although the whole concern of this book is with the more effective use of time available it would be unrealistic to argue that every study should be completed precisely within one, two, or three years. Students have, therefore, the problem of trying to schedule the transition from study to employment under conditions of some uncertainty. Few prospective employers are prepared to give an open-ended undertaking that will allow the student to complete his research before taking up an appointment. Rather more will allow some time to be spent during the early months of employment on completing the study, and in some instances (for example, educational appointments) the student may feel that he will be able to make time available. Our experience has shown that the completion of research within, say, six months of taking up an appointment is extremely rare. Despite every intention the demands of a (presumably) responsible position preclude other types of activity. This is a major reason why the completion rates reported by the research councils and commented upon in Chapter 1 have been so poor. Erstwhile full-time students discover that research is not something which can be easily picked up at any time and one consequence is that the longer the period taken the lower the probability of completion.

It is difficult for the young student to make a choice between what might be an attractive job opportunity and the completion of a degree. The short term attraction of a high salary compared with perhaps six months at subsistence level working on the completion of a thesis is difficult to resist. But whatever the economic climate the possession of a research degree is likely to continue to enhance the prospects of employment.

The part-time student will quite probably experience a change in employment during his studies, and each change of circumstances is likely to affect his schedules detrimentally. For this reason he needs to push ahead rapidly whenever work pressures allow. The only way to ensure that research work does not cause conflict when a plum posting is offered is to have completed it.

A rather different employment effect of which research degree students must take note is the increasingly difficult job situation of the early 1980s. Whereas until recent times students working for, say, doctorates could be sanguine about their prospects they must now be prepared to spend considerable time searching for employment. This can have a very damaging effect on schedules during the later part of their research when it is likely that most of their contingency allocation will have been used up. It is therefore sensible that extra time should be incorporated within the research plan to accommodate activities such as the preparation of job applications and attendance at interviews.

Supervisor Related Problems

Ideally a student should relate to one supervisor throughout his project. For students undertaking two or three year projects there exists, however, the possibility that staff mobility will prevent this from being achieved. In these circumstances the supervisor has a responsibility for ensuring that new arrangements are made which will have as little effect as possible upon the progress of the research. If the supervisor is staying in academic life it may be possible for the student to change from one institution to another (research councils will permit this). For a variety of reasons the student may be unwilling or unable to accept a transfer and in these circumstances the supervisor and his colleagues should endeavour to effect a move to another member of staff who is able to satisfy the range of requirements. Obviously the host institution will carry responsibility whatever the reason (for example, retirement, death in service) for the breaking of a supervisory arrangement.

In the unfortunate event that no suitable alternative supervisor can be found the student may be faced with the choice of continuing to work with nominal supervision only, ceasing his research, or making an application to another institution.

It is sometimes the case that a supervisor has not all the necessary skills to advise the student. This may be encountered during the analysis phase when knowledge of mathematical, statistical, or computing techniques are required. It is to be hoped that the supervisor will not attempt to conceal his ignorance in such matters as these and will direct the student to the appropriate quarters. The student should, however, never be diffident about approaching other members of staff, at the same time keeping his supervisor informed.

Thesis committees are an effective way in the longer research project of revealing areas that have not received sufficient attention during supervisory meetings and many institutions use them on a regular basis for this reason. No matter how excellent the working relationship it is rare at the doctoral level at least that every need of the student is recognised by the supervisor or that the supervisor is in a position to respond effectively to every request for assistance. Often the help needed from outsiders is small – a key reference, a suggestion as to methods of analysis – nonetheless it can well be of major benefit. The thesis committee therefore provides an excellent way of supplementing supervision and in addition may lead to the uncovering of serious difficulties of the type discussed below.

The most regrettable situation arises when a supervisor falls below what is acceptable in terms of both the quality and quantity of supervision. The traditional British 'apprentice model' is so dependent upon an effective relationship between student and supervisor that there must be a 'fall-back' position to which the former can resort. If he feels that his research progress is being marred for this reason he should not hesitate to take informal and then, if necessary, formal steps in an attempt to resolve the situation. All of this assumes that the supervisor has not responded to 'management' and may involve the matter being taken successively higher in the institutional hierarchy in order to find a workable solution. Action of this type, though unpalatable, may if not taken by the student adversely affect his career prospects.

Research Problems

The typical research project involves many stages and the chances of running into a snag somewhere along the way are, in the longer project at least, fairly high. The aim of this section is to discuss research problems that may be encountered and, where possible, ways by which they may be overcome. The latter may range from straightforward rectification of small defects to a major reinterpretation of what the research is about. Clearly the latter end of the spectrum of solutions is only relevant to those carrying out research at the master's level and above.

Two categories of research problem are proposed, those which threaten the continuation of the study and those which seriously delay the study.

1. **Threats to the Continuation of the Study** Although the future can never be predicted with certainty students who set out on research studies will normally expect (particularly if they have undertaken thorough topic analyses and/or research proposals) to achieve a successful outcome. To some degree the prospects of success are related to the

level and duration, and also the nature of the research (see Chapter 1), with the basic types of research and certain kinds of applied research being more risky in that conclusions which are novel are sought. All types of research may, however, be brought to a halt by factors outside the control of the student. These factors include the realisation that substantial conclusions cannot be drawn, the withdrawal of facilities, or evidence that some other researcher has successfully covered the same ground.

If the researcher finds that his efforts are likely to be fruitless there is little point in reminding him that his research design should have been more symmetrical with a low probability of an inconclusive outcome. For example, a student in the marketing area may have felt quite confident of achieving a valuable outcome from a study of the importance of attitudes of potential customers in relation to the promotion of different makes of car. Having collected a large volume of data and having subjected it to analysis he may remain unsure as to whether any relationship exists; an outcome which would be unacceptable.

In terms of the model of research presented in Chapter 2 the problem in this situation is one where the research has insufficient value. Major changes will therefore probably need to be made to the line of the research and the way it has been viewed, if a rescue is to be effected. These include examining why success was not achieved when it was expected, possibly by going outside the original field of research and relating it to other theories, or alternatively showing that similar assumptions to those underlying the original research are widely employed by practitioners and pointing out the consequences of their erroneous use. Thus in the present case the student might well attempt to explore other dimensions of the buying process. Perhaps his lack of success is explicable in terms of the high percentage of cars purchased by companies rather than by individuals? Alternatively if he can show that car design is strongly influenced by similar (incorrect) beliefs then his research has strong implications for the design policy of car manufacturers and this may well make a sufficiently weighty set of findings.

The withdrawal of facilities will primarily affect research studies which depend upon external co-operation. For example, an organisation which hitherto had been collaborating by permitting access to its Research and Development Department may decide to withdraw from the arrangement. In such cases the important question to be resolved is how far the value of the research is dependent on the resource concerned. It is easy to forget as commitment to a particular path of research develops the extent to which expediency dictated earlier choices; the support of a company with which the institution has close links; a private collection situated near to the researcher's home. On the other hand neither is necessarily unique and there may well be other possibilities of carrying out essentially the original research plan but using some other resource. Alternatively it may be possible to adopt a comparative stance in the research, for example, by looking at several other organisations and seeing how they cope with similar problems to those studied in the original company or by examining how one sequence of events uncovered in the examination of family papers impinged on others who were involved in them.

A more insidious problem than withdrawal of key resources is their inability to function as planned. Most engineering laboratories have test rigs that have either never worked at all or have at least required several generations of research students to get them to perform as intended. Computer software still refuses surprisingly often to work in accordance with its specification when moved from one computer to another. The difficulty here is that while the student can clearly see that tomorrow the hoped for results will emerge, in the meantime he has little to show for his efforts. Sooner or later, therefore, it is necessary to call a halt and make a decision as to whether to change the direction of the research and focus on getting the resource to function as planned. At the master's level and below this is frequently a sensible strategy since this work will probably be of an acceptable standard. At the doctoral level this is more rarely the case and so the decision will probably be to treat the resource as if withdrawn, in which case the earlier remarks apply.

Despite the increasing efficiency of information transfer it is still possible that two researchers will be covering, in ignorance, the same ground simultaneously. If this proves to be so when basic research with its emphasis on generalisability is involved there may be little that the 'second past the post' can do about it. There are however, relatively few situations where the difficulties are so extreme. Even in mathematics, which might seem the most likely area for it to be so, there is usually scope for alternative methods of deriving results. In the experimental sciences confirmatory evidence would be considered very desirable and in most situations in the social sciences and humanities exact and irremediable overlap is most unlikely. Much more likely is that the research provides an alternative view.

In each of the above cases the student researcher may initially feel that the ground has fallen away from under him. This will be the case particularly if more than fifty per cent of the period of the study has been completed. Given the catastrophe that appears to have befallen him it is unlikely that the judgement of the researcher will be sound. His primary need is for detached, expert advice from outsiders. The first source of help is the supervisor, but it is the nature of these problems that he may be too closely involved to proffer impartial guidance. Usually a better plan is for the student to discuss his problem informally with a variety of acquaintances who are also involved in research and then to convene an *(ad hoc)* thesis committee which is primarily composed of researchers with a proven ability in the field of research design who can offer a variety of perspectives on his problem. Ideally they should all be familiar with his field of research but have related rather than similar interests. Such a committee needs to focus on whether (a) there is a serious problem and (b) if so, can it be overcome with as little waste of previous work as possible? Where the answer to question (b) is 'no' the positive options open to the student would seem to be as follows:

a) try to define rapidly a new research topic which will have as much overlap as possible with the redundant topic;
b) consider conversion (in the case of the doctoral student) to an acceptable master's thesis;
c) drop the idea of completing a research degree and write as many papers as possible on the research completed for both academic and (if appropriate) professional journals;
d) write a book on the research area instead.

Much will depend on how much research time is left and on the enthusiasm which the student can retain. The experience gained from undertaking some of the customary research stages should be of considerable benefit if the student has to retrace his steps. Which of the options listed is to be preferred will depend on the individual but if at least one year of the study period remains consideration should be given to the working up of a new topic despite the knowledge that it may be necessary to write up a large part of the thesis on a part-time basis.

It is not easy to make more than general recommendations on the development of a new topic as so much depends on the line of research which has been abandoned. Nor is it suggested that the latter is a common experience. The student might however comfort himself with the thought that the greater the experience he has gained the easier it should be to both define and follow a new direction of study.

One situation in which consolation may be derived from the frustration of a study arises when a student working for a doctorate has done sufficient work to satisfy the requirements of a master's degree. Much depends on the student's objectives, if he sees his future in tertiary education or in research he may be more inclined to use the time remaining at his disposal to work towards a redefined doctorate. If not the prospect of a master's degree may be more appealing.

There are few students who would accept that there should be no tangible outcome of, perhaps three years of study but would see as desirable the establishment of a reputation primarily through publication in academic journals, and perhaps a measure of lecturing or consultancy. If, therefore, the student has made substantial progress but has fallen short of the requirements of a PhD the acceptance of a few well-written papers by academic journals of standing may offer some compensation. In any event research students are unlikely to communicate with the world at large through their thesis and if it is an academic reputation they seek they must be prepared to write either books or papers or both.

2. Some Causes of Serious Delay

The above comments refer to circumstances in which a particular course of study is terminated for unpredicted reasons. More frequently encountered and linked to poor rates of research degree completion are studies which are significantly delayed not so much by inefficient research management but by the occurrence of a specific problem.

The most usual hurdle to be overcome faces students who have collected large volumes of data but who are unable to analyse it in sufficient depth. This reinforces the argument that the type of analysis to be employed should be anticipated as much as possible and explains why in this book data analysis precedes data collection.

It is to be hoped that constructive advice will be available from the supervisor on analytical approaches but it should be recognised that in many instances he may not possess the requisite skills. If this is so the student should not be diffident about seeking assistance from other sources. The academic world has within it many people who can provide guidance and it is a measure of the student's initiative to be able to make effective contact. What can almost be guaranteed is that assistance will be forthcoming on request. This requires that students should be prepared to leave their desks and perhaps undertake some travel, but the effort should be worthwhile.

Another major cause of delay arises from dependence on other peoples' reactions to a researcher's initiatives. The estimated duration of activities used to develop schedules in Chapter 3 assume 'normal' speeds of response but from time to time this will not be achieved. There may be lengthy delays in gaining approval from a collaborating body, items of equipment may not be delivered on time, questionnaires sent out for pilot test may not be returned and so on. The risk is largely the extent to which parts of the study lie outside the direct control of the student. If there is much of this the need to adopt a formalised approach to planning can only be stressed. It is not so much a matter of normal 'lead time' (the interval between requesting something to be done and its occurrence) but a matter of considering in advance of a specific request whether the ground can be prepared in any way. For example, it would be worthwhile determining the frequency of meetings of an external body which will give approval for a study to be undertaken, or when a key individual is likely to take his holidays, or whether an alternative supplier for a piece of equipment can be identified.

The consequences of delays such as those caused by some aspect of the process of the research or the research design may, it is to be hoped, be absorbed during the remainder of the study. But if delay is substantial a student working for a research degree may have to resort to the second and third options (conversion, if appropriate, to a master's degree, or writing papers instead) mentioned above. Although failure to achieve the prime objective is to be regretted it is highly desirable that there should be some lasting indication of the student's efforts.

General Support Problems

This category includes those problems which arise neither from the individual, his supervisor, nor the research itself. The vast majority of students who commence a research study do so in the expectation that sufficient support will be available for them to achieve their objectives. Thus they anticipate that appropriate funds will be forthcoming and that at the least they will be provided with minimum facilities such as desk space. Most students would not consider doing full-time research unless funding were guaranteed for the expected period of their study and the sensible student will have established what will be available in terms of accommodation, telephone, filing space, laboratory, library, and computer facilities and so on. The question is whether there is a possibility that any of this support will be withdrawn or will prove to be insufficient.

Students with grants can normally expect to receive, in real terms, a similar level of financial support throughout their studies. The only major problem that might arise under this heading would occur if the execution of the research involved activities that did not qualify for funding (for example the transcription of interview tapes, or overseas travel). Lack of foresight by the student would at the least require that he should be able to meet such expenditure from other sources.

If financial support is provided by other types of organisation there may be some risk of discontinuation. This has been a not uncommon occurrence for students from developing countries when political changes have led to a withdrawal of grants. In the UK many students are funded by private sector organisations and although we are unaware of such incidents it is conceivable that economic recession and company closure could lead to similar problems arising.

Many institutions of further and higher education have 'hardship committees' which are often able to give practical support to those students who for no fault of their own find that sponsorship is withdrawn, but this may be limited to fees only.

Although suppport problems are dominated by issues relating to fees or grants some students continue to experience difficulties through the data collection and analysis stages. Costs and facilities associated with the former should be capable of reasonable estimation and should be highlighted during the assessment of topic feasibility. Thus questions as to whether funds will be available to purchase equipment and materials, to cover travel, or to pay for the mailing of several hundreds of questionnaires will need to be resolved. Less easy to assess will be whether appropriate support for analysis will be forthcoming. Many students rely heavily on advice from computing departments and it is wise to anticipate as far as is possible the likely extent of what will be needed. Lengthy delays may arise if the student does nothing until he is on the point of requiring analysis to be undertaken. In large part, therefore, this type of problem should be anticipated at the planning stage and should not fall into the 'unavoidable or unexpected category'. Usually, for example, ample notification will be given of the upgrading of a computer system so that students will be able to reschedule their analysis if facilities are to be temporarily withdrawn or make alternative arrangements if software becomes unavailable.

WORKING WITH A SUPERVISOR

In view of the desirability and importance of high quality supervision of student research projects it is felt that comments are apposite at this point on the type of working relationship which ideally should operate. It is assumed that (at least for research degree students) the supervisor satisfies all of the requirements listed in Chapter 2 and that the student sees a reasonable prospect of a satisfactory relationship. If he does not then he should not hesitate to attempt to find an alternative.

In the initial stages of his research, at least, the student should look to his supervisor for guidance as to appropriate standards. Since this is an emotive aspect of research a word of warning is necessary. Many supervisors see their role in standard setting as advisory and do not feel it appropriate to direct the student as to what needs to be done to achieve the right level. Rather they see themselves as indicating directions through comments or queries and if these are disregarded they may, eventually, cease to make them. The student, therefore, must make sure that he attempts to meet points which are raised since his relationship with his supervisor will otherwise suffer.

As will be apparent the supervisor is seen as fulfilling a number of key roles in any research project, though naturally the balance varies depending on the level of research. In general a supervisor should:

(a) get the student to define objectives at each stage of his work;
(b) check to see that those objectives are met;
(c) verify with the student that his work is of the right standard.

In practice these three aims will normally necessitate a fair amount of guidance as the inevitable snags are encountered. The topic of how best to ensure that guidance is obtained is now examined.

Proposed below is what is seen as the ideal supervisory arrangements in the certain knowledge that the actual outcome will, probably, fall short of this. The relationship from the full-time student's point of view is also focused upon, although it is hoped that the suggestions will make sense to the supervisor. The reasons for concentrating on the full-time research student are that he will normally be supported by some grant-awarding body, which, as pointed out in Chapter 1, will increasingly be interested in seeing that the students it supports, complete their research degrees within the period nominally required. Given that this changes the pressures on both institution and supervisor it also implies greater conformity on the part of the full-time student than might have been the case in a more relaxed era. Accordingly the recommendations to the student are fairly strongly prescriptive. It is suggested that both student or supervisor may find them useful in negotiating at its outset the type of relationship they expect to be maintained.

Though for stylistic reasons the term 'supervisor' is still referred to most of what is said applies equally well where the student has more than one supervisor. In fact it may well be that there are relatively few individual supervisors who measure up to the ideal portrayed here. Indeed, those who do may well suffer from an embarrassingly large number of requests for supervision, and under these circumstances might insist on an additional supervisor being appointed to share the task.

It is recommended that the student should:

1. attempt at the outset to ascertain the supervisor's views of the staff/student relationship;
2. agree with the supervisor the routine aspects of the relationship (and take responsibility for their implementation);

3. produce written lists of queries prior to meetings with the supervisor;
4. keep written notes of meetings with the supervisor and submit copies to him;
5. agree with the supervisor the nature and timing of written material to be submitted to him.

Each of these points will be discussed in turn.

1. Even though both student and supervisor find a mutual interest in the research the relationship can be soured if, in particular, there are a number of counts on which the supervisor has strong feelings. If, for example, the supervisor has high standards of punctuality, the relationship would rapidly deteriorate if a student was persistently late in keeping appointments or broke them altogether. Similarly then it is very desirable that a student should be able to knock on the door of his supervisor, but if the latter prefers that arrangements should be made by telephone or through a secretary then this procedure should be adhered to.

2. Regular contact between student and supervisor is very desirable. It is accepted that a small proportion of students may have sufficient competence and motivation to complete even a doctorate unaided, but the large majority will rely heavily on expert guidance, mainly from the supervisor. In the latter respect a prime requirement is that the supervisor should not lose touch with progress. It should, therefore, be agreed that the interval between meetings should not exceed a certain period. At some stages of the research frequent discussions will be required but ideally routine contact should be maintained with the interval between meetings not exceeding two weeks. The supervisor has a definite responsibility to comply with such an arrangement but as the person to suffer if regular contact breaks down is the student it is he who should take the initiative in rearranging dates if a meeting has to be postponed.

3. It is helpful to the supervisor if the student submits a brief list of any queries or problems before routine meetings. This serves a number of purposes; it provides a basic agenda for the meeting; it forces the student to properly define what might otherwise remain a vague, unvoiced unease; it prevents the accretion of small difficulties into a single insuperable obstacle, and it fulfils a primary need for successful project management, namely the recognition of problems that need to be resolved. Obviously in many types of research the student will also need to bring along to meetings supplementary material such as questionnaires or laboratory reports that bear on the queries raised.

4. Something positive should emerge from most meetings between student and supervisor. This may take the form of questions answered or

suggestions to follow. It is all too easy to assume that these will be remembered but the nature of research makes it quite probable that they will not be. Whether or not the supervisor keeps his own written record of meetings the student should certainly do so. Those students who have an aversion to the methodical should learn to accommodate their feelings on this point even to the extent of providing their supervisor with a copy of notes of meeting.

5. Apart from written records of meetings maintained at the initiative of the student it is wise for the latter to gain some idea of the demands for other written material which the supervisor will make upon him. These will fall into he categories of a) progress reports and b) draft chapters.

The student should be prepared to submit progress reports at a frequency as high as once per month until the writing-up phase proper of the research is entered. They should be as succinct as possible unless the supervisor requests that a particular issue should be enlarged upon.

Progress reports should record what work has been done since the previous report and show the relationship of this work to the following:

a)   the latest version of the research plan;
b)   whether a milestone event in the project has been reached;
c)   action points agreed at the last progress meeting;
d)   queries raised by the student or suggestions from the supervisor at routine meetings in the intervening period.

Where necessary the assumptions on which the work is based and the ways it was checked should be clearly laid out. This makes it possible to verify at each stage that the work is of the requisite quality and should avoid the disastrous discovery in the final stages that it is based on untenable assumptions. The submission of progress reports is the primary mechanism by which the student ensures that his research plan remains feasible or discovers when it needs amendment. Most successfully managed research projects use some similar formal device as indicated in Chapter 3.

Supervisors vary in the pressure they put on their students to draft out chapters of the report at an early stage in the research. Table 3.1 and figures 3.1, and 3.3 are based on a research plan in which the writing of draft chapters is seen to be realistic after only four weeks of the execution phase. What might be attempted here is the 'Introduction' or 'Background to the Research'. In large part the writing may ultimately be redundant due to a shift in the direction of the research or simply by becoming out of date. The major advantages are that the supervisor will be able to assess and react to the content of the material submitted to him, and that the student will be able to gauge the magnitude of the writing-up task, at the same time coming to grips with the demands of format and style.

An obvious point which applies to the submission of any written material is that the supervisor should have had the opportunity of reading it before he meets the student.

Thus far the assumption has been that the student is working with a single supervisor. As pointed out earlier, however, it may be desirable to appoint a second, or indeed the institution may require it. At its best such a supervisory relationship can be of considerable benefit to the student. The calibre of advice that he receives and the additional scrutiny given to the work increase his chance of turning out high quality work. On the other hand such a relationship can create problems that do not exist with a single supervisor. It is easy for each supervisor to believe that the other is carrying the main weight of the supervision. It is more difficult to organise meetings at which both supervisors can be present and additional copies of written material need to be prepared. It follows then that to gain the full benefit of such an arrangement will ususally involve the student in more managerial effort.

This section has been written to advise students how they can get the best out of their supervisor. They should remember, however, that although their research may constitute the whole world as far as they are concerned, this will not be so in the case of their supervisor. Nevertheless, most supervisors are more likely to respond positively and effectively if they are to some extent 'managed' and the student should not be diffident about adopting the courses of action described above.

THE POSITIVE VIEW OF RESEARCH PROGRESS

Virtually the whole of this chapter has been concerned with problems which the research student may encounter, suggesting perhaps that the successful completion of a research project is comparable with the crossing of a minefield. Whilst it is felt that the student should be aware of various types of pitfall and subscribe to the notion that to be forewarned is to be forearmed there is much that can be done to promote progress and that has been the primary aim of this chapter.

Even though a student may have drawn up a research schedule he should not be complacent about being on course. If he sees an opportunity for completing a stage more rapidly than planned he should do this, and if the saving is significant the schedule should be amended. Many degrees are of fixed duration, this being determined by written examinations. If, however, a research student is able to complete a study more quickly than planned little is gained by utilising all of the originally intended period. Though average completion periods are high (four to five years for doctorates) some students finish in relatively short times and this has obvious advantages. Even if students are ahead of schedule for a limited period only, this will have reduced the likely demand on the time set aside for contingencies and will thus increase the probability of completing on time.

The prime evidence of progress is the writing of parts of the research report. Wherever possible the student should commence writing draft chapters quite early in the study. Although this comment is more relevant to the longer studies it is an approach which should be adopted whenever possible. By doing this, in addition to resolving issues of style, tangible evidence of progress will be accumulated. As the research progresses the variance between the first and final draft should reduce markedly.

Student research has been separated into a number of distinct phases, with 'execution' falling between the finalising of the research proposal and writing up. This has been largely for convenience of discussion and as has been pointed out on a number of occasions there is in practice much overlap of activity. As far as the student is concerned he will be executing his research from commencement to the moment when he submits his thesis, dissertations, or report. In many cases the research will be the student's sole academic activity although there will no doubt be many other competing demands on his time. There is much to suggest that despite the fact that successful completion of a study is vital to the self-esteem and career prospects of students, research activities are from time-to-time ranked much lower than they ought to be. It is not too facile to state that during his period of study his life should be built around his research and that only in exceptional circumstances should a conscious decision be taken to delay a stage of the research in favour of doing something else. The exercising of tight control of carefully planned procedures is much more likely to produce the desired results than is an approach which sees research as something to be done when circumstances permit.

SUMMARY

RESEARCH RARELY PROCEEDS SMOOTHLY: The student will encounter and, if he is to be successful, must overcome a range of problems.

MANY PROBLEMS ARE AVOIDABLE: Careful planning should highlight this type of problem. Two aspects, over-commitment and supervisory arrangements, should be given much consideration.

UNEXPECTED PROBLEMS MAY ARISE: These may relate to the student, the supervisor, the research, or support for it.

RESEARCH PROGRESS CAN BE FACILITATED: by continually adopting a positive attitude towards it and identifying and pursuing activities which are consistent with effective and timely completion.

8

Presentation Of The Research Findings

INTRODUCTION

The evaluation of student research is nearly always made through an assessment of the written account of the work undertaken and the conclusions reached. In addition the student is often required to explain or defend verbally his findings. This chapter will be concerned with the two aspects and will consider the steps which need to be taken to ensure that both written and verbal presentation satisfy requirements.

At the beginning of this book it was stated that it was the aim to provide guidance for degree students at all levels who were required, as part of their course, to complete a project. The range thus extends from the undergraduate student who has one or two months in which to

174

conduct and report on a project to the doctoral student who has three years of full-time study at his disposal. The same policy will, however, continue to apply in this chapter as elsewhere, namely that advice will be given on the preparation and presentation of a doctoral thesis with only occasional comments on the needs at other levels.

Figure 8.1 lists criteria by which the quality of reports on student research may be judged. The figure is consistent with earlier commentary in which the general requirements of research at different levels were indicated. All institutions empowered to confer degrees publish regulations for the guidance of candidates but it is difficult for the student to glean what precisely is required of him. It is not easy to identify a sharp divide between the levels and in the absence of sound advice from a supervisor the written account may fall short of or exceed requirements by a substantial margin. Most institutions do not attempt a comparison between requirements at different levels and even if this is made the outcome may not be very helpful. For example in 1980 a criterion for the degree of Master of Philosophy at the University of East Anglia was that 'the extent of the subject will normally be rather narrower and the degree of attainment rather less than is expected of a candidate for the degree of Doctor of Philosophy'. It would appear that if the student is able to satisfy himself that the criteria listed in Figure 8.1 for his particular level are met the requisite standard will be satisfied.

Regardless as to whether the written accounts are theses, dissertations, or reports consideration will need to be given to the structure; style of writing; and process and content.

It should be noted (to borrow an ice skating analogy) that each of these aspects and particularly the structure and the process and content embodies both 'compulsory' elements which require the student to conform to some standard and 'free' elements where the student can display his own approach. Thus under compulsory elements the need to observe certain typographical standards, for example, that text be typed double-spaced with at least 1½ inch margins should be noted. Similarly the work of others must be properly referenced and some institutions may even prescribe the form that citation of particular types of work such as journal articles should take.

Where dissertations and theses are involved the student should have a right to expect a guidance manual to be available which will state requirements on such matters as binding, appendices, margins, figures, and pictures. Probably the most effective way of coming to grips with such requirements is for a student to scrutinise theses of dissertations in his library. It is possible with the introduction of new courses which include a research element that students may not have access to completed reports in their own institution and indeed may find little formal guidance available. If this is the case they may find it of benefit to visit a convenient university library and decide upon their own structure to put forward for adoption at their own institution.

However, the research reports produced by students who were successful in the past can for a variety of reasons be an imperfect guide to present standards. Modestly written reports may have been redeemed by a brilliant defence at an oral examination. The standards of the field may have changed as more research has been done. The student's best guide to the adequacy of his own report is therefore the degree to which it conforms to the requirements laid down in the regulations of the institution and the detailed criteria for evaluating a report given later.

Structure and style are examined first as it is important that the student should be able to manage the process of writing in the knowledge of what is required of him. Structure is held to include the physical characteristics and main components of the written presentation. In large part these will be defined by the regulations of his institution or by the logical breakdown and order consistent with a reasoned account of research work. Within any requirements more or less imposed upon him the student has much discretion as to the 'style' of writing and this aspect is given separate consideration as the impact which the writing makes will largely depend on style.

REPORT STRUCTURE

The student most not lose sight of the prime aim of writing up his research which is to convince examiners that he has satisfied the appropriate criteria contained in Figure 8.1. He is not, therefore, writing for the world at large but, in the first instance, for one or two individuals who will be acting for the institution or the degree awarding body in the examining process. The student must structure his writing in such a way that his research is presented in the most effective manner and must at the same time comply with any requirements which the institution lays down.

Other than listing criteria against which writings will be evaluated institutions give little indication in their regulations of what is needed in terms of structure. A question frequently asked by students is 'How long should it be?'. The only real answer to this question at doctoral level is that the thesis should be of sufficient length to accommodate everything which is needed for the student to discuss and prove within context any proposition which he puts forward. An examination of university library

LEVEL	DESCRIPTION	CRITERIA
First degrees and some master's degrees which require the completion of a project.	Project report	1. A well structured and convincing account of a study, the resolution of a problem, or the outcome of an experiment.
Master's degree by study and dissertation	Dissertation	1. An ordered, critical and reasoned exposition of knowledge gained through the student's efforts 2. Evidence of awareness of the literature
Master's degree by research	Thesis	1. Evidence of an original investigation or the testing of ideas 2. Competence in independent work or experimentation 3. An understanding of appropriate techniques 4. Ability to make critical use of published work and source materials 5. Appreciation of the relationship of the special theme to the wider field of knowledge 6. Worthy, in part, of publication
Doctoral degree	Thesis	1. to 6. as for Master's degree by research 7. Originality as shown by the topic researched or the methodology employed 8. Distinct contribution to knowledge

Figure 8.1   Criteria to be satisfied by reports on student research

shelves will show the wide variations in length which have arisen in order to satisfy this general requirement. Experience has however indicated that the vast majority of successful doctoral theses do not exceed 500 pages of A4 size typed in double-spacing on one side only. Because of a tendency of some research students towards 'overkill' some universities now place an upper limit on wordage which may be 100,000 or even lower for PhDs with master's theses being restricted perhaps to 60,000 words.[1] At approximately 250 words per A4 page a 100,000 word thesis of about 400 pages, is under half the length of some of the longer theses to be found.

There is a logical order with which (subject to variations imposed by local regulations) most written reports on research should conform:

Title page
Preface
Contents
List of Tables
List of Figures
List of other types of materials
Chapters
Appendices
List of references
Bibliography
Index

All of these sections need not necessarily appear. Undergraduate reports for example may include only the title page, contents and chapters. Because of the need to relate the research to a body of knowledge a list of references will be a vital element of master's and doctoral theses. Such a list will include all relevant works which have been consulted by the author and which have been cited in the text. A distinction is made between a list of references and a bibliography where the latter is supplied as a comprehensive coverage of books and journals in an area, even though these may not have been cited in the text. Most theses will not carry a bibliography or an index unless the author has publication in mind.

The preface, which precedes the contents, is an important feature of most written accounts and will be discussed in the section dealing with content. Students are often confused by the difference between a table

1. Both Edinburgh University and the University of East Anglia require that PhD theses shall not normally exceed 100,000 words. Corresponding limits for M Phil theses at these two universities are 60,000 and 65,000 words respectively.

and a figure. The simplest rule is that apart from the descriptive margins tables are composed wholly of numerical data whereas, with certain exceptions, all other items of this form are figures. The exceptions are the 'other materials' mentioned in the above list which include such items as photographs or maps. Even in these latter cases serious objection could not be raised if they were viewed as figures, particularly if there were very few of them. It should be remembered that figures or tables which have not been originated by the writer should be acknowledged and full details of sources given.

Increasingly students wish to include computer output in their writings, and this will be discussed in more detail later. It is usually necessary to prune such output drastically and a decision is often needed as to whether selected pages should be incorporated as figures or whether larger quantities should be bound in as appendices or presented as a separate portfolio.

Citation and Quotation

A research report differs from many other forms of writing such as newspaper articles in that it should make clear what material and ideas have been originated by the student himself and what he owes to the work of others. On the matter of direct quotation it should be remembered that the requirements of Figure 8.1. suggest that at most levels of research it is important that the student shows that he has understood the ideas of others and this he can only do by demonstrating his ability to summarise them and present them within his own framework. This means that under most circumstances the amount of direct quotation should be fairly small. Obviously there are situations where direct quotation is necessary. A study of the impact of Kierkegaard on twentieth century writers on existentialism would be strange indeed without substantial quotations of Kierkegaard himself and sections of text from later authors that appear to have been influenced by him. Equally much theory in applied mathematics, say, is of such elegance that it would be foolish to rewrite it in a different notation. There is, however, rarely a case for the type of research report that consists mainly of quotations from various authors glued together by an occasional sentence supplied by the researcher.

Obviously quotations should be properly differentiated from the main body of the research report. Indented single spaced text is perhaps the easiest way of clearly differentiating the longer passage, though quotation marks are generally adequate for a single sentence. Variations such as different type faces may also be helpful. In either case the work from which the quotation is drawn should be clearly referenced as discussed below.

Where other authors are drawn on for ideas rather than direct quotation, things can be a little more difficult. Many ideas are in the public domain so that if the researcher is to avoid infelicities such as: 'Most chairs have four legs (Adam, 1775; Chippendale, 1778). Similar tendencies have been noted in tables (Hepplewhite, 1782; Sheraton, 1804)' he needs to observe certain rules about referencing other work. To some extent this must depend on the customs of the field in which he is writing. On the whole, though, a defensible approach would be to reference only those ideas which an inexpert reader might think were the researchers even though they are not. In such cases the researcher should try to give the original source of the idea provided this can be done without affectation and also the place where he himself found it, which may, of course be different. Thus if the researcher has become familiar with, for instance, information theory and the work of Shannon through reading someone else's introduction, academic courtesy would seem to dictate a formula such as: 'As Brillouin's account of Shannon's (1947) work shows (*Science and Information Theory*, 1962) the theory of information has much in common with ideas from fields of physics such as thermodynamics'.

The way in which the work in question is cited must, of course, comply with whatever standards are prescribed by the institution. Often these allow considerable latitude, however. The point made in Chapter 4 may be recalled, namely that it takes little longer to supply all relevant details in the list of references than to use only an abbreviated form of reference. As far as citation in the body of the text is concerned there are two broad schemes in use: the Harvard method as followed in this book (basically author + date) or the numerical approach in which each reference is given a specific number. The former approach is simpler and permits the insertion or deletion of references at will, whereas in the latter case any references which are introduced or deleted at a later stage will necessitate all of the subsequent numbers being changed. On the other hand, the Harvard method is cumbersome if a particular page is to be referenced.

Flexibility is desirable within the two schemes mentioned, and is linked to style which will be discussed below. Thus emphasis may be given to the idea or to the author:

a) A strong claim is made that a system of equity must exist within every society (Usher, D., 1981);

or b) Usher (1981) has argued that every society should have within it a system of equity.

It will be noted that in alternative b) the initial has not been included. If this might lead to confusion as in the case of numerous Smiths being cited, it would be sensible to supply the surname plus one or more christian names, for example, Adam Smith.

If the author adopts the numerical approach he may still prefer to make reference to a name. For example:

 i) Usher argued in 1981[14] that every society should have within it a system of equity

may be preferred to:

 ii) It has been argued[14] that . . .

where, of course, the reference number is [14].

An advantage of a), b), and i) is that if the student is drawing heavily on the ideas of an author he will, for as long as the thread remains unbroken, be able to introduce the surname of the author without repeating date, initials, or perhaps the title of the work cited.

In addition to the need within the body of the text to confirm that the student is able to relate his thoughts to the body of knowledge he must also consider the link between individual references and the list which will be positioned at the end of his report. External examiners usually scrutinise the list of references very carefully and will be critical of lists which are not both comprehensive and well presented. If the numerical approach is adopted the text and reference can be linked easily in either direction. One limitation is that a reader may not be able to establish quickly whether a particular author has been referenced. With the author plus date approach someone reading through the list of references will not be able to turn immediately to that part of the text to establish what ideas have been taken from the author in question.

It should be apparent that with the author plus date approach the list of references will be presented in the form normally taken by bibliographies, namely that authors will be cited in alphabetical order. In some instances students adopt the latter approach for their reports as a whole but at the end of each chapter incorporate a separate list compiled in order of appearance.

A standard procedure should be adopted when citing bibliographical references, particularly in research theses. Students should request from their librarian advice as to which method to use. The prerequisite of any system is that the reference should supply sufficient and unambiguous detail. In the main, books and journal articles will be referenced and a commonly employed approach is:

a) for books: author and initials (in capitals), title of book, (under-lined or in italics), place of publisher, publication, date, pages referenced;

b) for articles: author and initials (in capitals), title of article in quotes, name of journal (underlined or in italics), volume number, issue, pages referenced, year.

There will be occasions when other types of reference are made: for example to theses and separately authored chapters in books. Useful guidance on these and other matters may be obtained from British Standard 5605 (1978), 'Recommendations for Citing Publications by Bibliographic References'.

Certain latin words and phrases encountered in scholarly works can be useful in referencing. Sometimes a student may wish to quote something which contains an obvious, grammatical, typographical, or numerical error. In this case 'sic' typed within brackets and placed immediately after the error will point to its origin.

It was suggested above that if the student wishes to make a lengthy and unbroken reference to an author the latter's surname may be used from time to time in the text without involving addition to the list of references. If, however, the points taken from the source are widely scattered or if other authors are cited in between the following latin phrases can help in reducing the bulk of the reference list:

a) Ibidem (abbreviated to ibid.): in the same work allowing successive reference to the same work. This replaces all details in the previous reference, but should be followed by page number.

b) Opere citato (abbreviated to op. cit.): in the work cited. This required the author's name and page number, and refers to a work already cited.

c) Loco citato (abbreviated to loc. cit.): in the place cited. This is used with the author's name and is similar to op. cit. but is more precise as it refers to the same passage in a book already cited.

An example of the use of the three phrases is as follows:

BYNON, T., *Historical Linguistics,* Cambridge University Press, Cambridge, 1977, p. 86.
FOWLER R., *Understanding Language,* Routledge, London, 1974, p.31.
Ibid., p.50. (a reference to the *previous* book – Fowler).
BYNON, T., loc. cit. (a reference to the *same* work and *same* page).
BYNON, T., op. cit. p.14. (a reference to the *same* book, but a *different* page).

Doctoral theses often contain several hundreds of references and the work involved in ensuring that these are systematically presented and are error free can be formidable. There are obvious advantages at this level of using bibliographic software of the type referred to in Chapter 4 or of utilising some of the facilities of word processing which will be discussed later in this chapter.

STYLE OF WRITING

The development of an appropriate style (the quality of writing) can be a demanding task for research students. It is unlikely that more than a small proportion will have made a particular study of the written form of the English language and many are disinclined to allocate time to such an activity, preferring instead to react to comments from their supervisor. If the supervisor is able to give advice on style this approach may work but if not (or if in the case of shorter projects the work is largely unsupervised) the ultimate written account, perhaps weak in other aspects, may fail because it is not easily readable.

Cooper (1965) observes that 'Writers of reports are fortunately not in the extreme situation of having to satisfy millions of readers to stay in business. If they were they would probably starve'. A short time spent in developing style will be of much benefit both in writing about the research and later in life when it is assumed that the ability to communicate will continue to be needed.

Much has been written about 'readability' and Cooper comments on action taken by government in the UK in response to the writings of Gowers (1954). Cooper also refers to a measure proposed by Gunning (1952) known as the 'fog index'. This description was used because it was felt that long words and sentences made for 'foggy' reading. Briefly:

Fog Index = 0.4 (Average sentence length + per cent of words more than two syllables in length)

Words that are capitalised, are combinations of short simple words, or, for example, arise because of the use of the past tense, are excluded from the calculation. According to Cooper, Gunning regarded a 'fog index' of twelve as the danger point, beyond which text becomes difficult to read. An analysis of the writings of classical and popular authors indicated that their fog index did not exceed twelve. Widely read magazines of the time such as *Time* and *Look* were reported as having a 'fog index' of ten and eight respectively, whereas one new highbrow magazine with an index well above twelve ceased to be published within a year.

As would be expected writers on style also express views on paragraph length. The general recommendation is that paragraphs should be short, not so much for clarity as for textual appearance. They should, however, be long enough to accommodate a particular idea and very short paragraphs of one or two sentences should be avoided both for reasons of appearance and to avoid the reader having to switch too rapidly from one point to another.

Attention to the suggestions made in this section will not guarantee good style. However, students should not be under the impression that there is a common style which they should seek to attain. Cooper (1965) states:

> Good style is one which makes some impact on the reader. The author's personality comes through. Poor style usually refers to writing which is involved, where there is little attempt to structure the writing, and usually where the vocabulary range is limited.

One aspect of style on which students often seek guidance is the use of personal pronouns. Because student projects are usually of a personal nature there is obviously much scope for 'I' to be used throughout the report. This may be avoided by the use of the passive voice; thus; 'It was found that . . .' is used instead of 'I found that . . .'. Traditionally, in most fields of research use of the passive voice has been favoured with the major exception being the use of 'we' in mathematics. In recent times however, limited use of the first person has been accepted, if only to break up the monotonous effect of continued use of the passive voice.

Writers on style such as Cooper and Broehl make a number of suggestions as to how impact may be increased. Thus Cooper (1965 pp 127–136) stresses the importance of analogy, metaphorical language, repetition for emphasis, rhythm, and the avoidance of cacophony and 'phoney' style. Broehl and Shurter (1965 pp 81–87) argue that writers should make effective use of verbs, be direct, use an appropriate tone, and be specific. Students should give consideration to suggestions of this type and should be aware of the pitfalls which result in poor style.

It may be useful to adopt as a model the writings of a specific author or of workers in a particular field such as economics that maintains a tradition of clear communication of technically difficult subjects. It should be remembered however that the research report is typically aimed at a narrower audience and that certain knowledge and predispositions on the part of the reader can be assumed. Thus though jargon would usually be frowned on in a text that was to have wide non-specialist readership it may be used in a research report in order that it be clear what the report is about, avoiding the ambiguities that are often associated with everyday language. Similar arguments apply to abbreviations, particularly to entities that have several word names that are mentioned frequently in the text, for example, UNESCO.

PROCESS AND CONTENT

It is assumed that by enquiry and reading the student will learn broadly what is required of him in terms of the way in which his report should be structured and presented and will be aware of factors which make for good or bad style. He will also have assembled through some of the steps described in Chapter 6 a substantial database, parts of which he will have subjected to analysis. By the later stages of his research he will have reached some conclusions and will probably feel under increasing pressure to start to convert all of this into a semblance of what ultimately will be his thesis or report.

It is argued that the process of writing up a thesis in particular is probably much more demanding than the average student envisages and to this end attempts to draft chapters as early in the research as is feasible plus the production of one or more journal articles in the course of a research degree is strongly favoured. This requires some elaboration of the 'chapters' portion of the outline structure of reports proposed above. Chapter headings should have been suggested by research degree students as part of their research proposal and will probably be consistent with the following logical order.

Introduction
Survey of prior research
Research design
Results of the research
Analysis
Summary and conclusions

Although the introductory chapter probably suffers more revision than any other the student should be encouraged to write this together with chapters which review the current state of knowledge and describe what the approach to their research will be.

It should be remembered that the order in which chapters are first written may not be the same as that in which they eventually appear in the report. As will presently be discussed the structuring of a report so that ideas appear in logical sequence is by no means easy. A device that is sometimes useful is to write one of the later chapters on some aspect of the analysis or the conclusions in order to obtain some feel for what needs to be introduced prior to this chapter. Where the research report is written over several months, however, it is most unlikely that certain chapters will not undergo major redrafting both because the researcher's ideas have matured and also to obtain a more logically structured argument.

There are two aspects at least to obtaining a logical structure. One might be dubbed tactical and involves the organisation of individual chapters in the most effective way. This will be discussed later. The other aspect is 'strategic', that is, obtaining a satisfactory interrelationship among the various chapters so that the report as a whole presents a coherent argument. In most research reports there is usually a considerable element of flexibility possible in defining the interrelationship between chapters and this is a frequent source of problems with material either being repeated in several places or never being properly presented anywhere. Thus if we consider a student research project that has been concerned with an in-depth study of the use of computer marketing models in four organisations, the end purpose of which is to suggest criteria that distinguish successful from unsuccessful applications, then at a minimum it would probably contain the following material:

1. Prior research on computer marketing models
2. Prior research on factors affecting the success of computer marketing models
3. Prior research on factors affecting the success of other computer models
4. Account of study in organisation A
5. Account of study in organisation B
6. Account of study in organisation C
7. Account of study in organisation D
8. Analysis of the individual case studies and construction of an overall scheme for the prediction of success
9. Conclusions

Though this breakdown is distinctly simpler than that on which the student would probably undertake his own research it illustrates the types of problems that occur. Firstly, it may be noted that before a list can be formulated at all many implicit decisions have to be made about topics that will not be explored. In this case, for example, no reference will apparently be made to the literature on the management of innovations *per se,* though this might well be relevant. Secondly, there are a number of problems on how this material should be combined into chapters. Should items 1 and 2 be combined into one chapter, probably the best way if the factors affecting success appear to be highly model specific, or should they be separated? If, however, the factors affecting success seem to be relatively independent of the model concerned there may well be a case for combining items 2 and 3. Similarly items 4, 5, 6 and 7 could be run in parallel through several chapters looking at applications of different types of model in each of the four organisations in turn or alternatively each item could form a single chapter. The most important determinant of the choice here should be the way in which the material will be analysed. For the moment, however, this particular aspect is left since similar problems will be discussed when we deal with the construction of individual chapters. This leaves one further important concern that will undoubtedly exercise the researcher as he comes to write his report, namely the degree to which he prepares the ground in earlier chapters for what is to come later. To take but two examples, some of the previous work on factors determining success will be highly relevant. Some of his field observations will be more appropriate than others. In either case it is sensible to highlight these particular aspects as they are dealt with so that the reader knows that he should pay especial attention to them.

Effective strategy in report writing requires that the student has a clear picture of the report as a whole. As indicated earlier, however, he will not usually evolve this until he has already written a great deal. In reality, then, it is not likely that the final result will closely resemble the initial structure proposed. The student should expect to have to reorganise some of his material and should therefore allow time for this in his planning.

The process of writing is interpretated broadly to include the following:

a) preparing to write;
b) the writing itself;
c) editing;
d) proofreading.

Preparing to Write

In one sense the whole period spent by a student on his research before he commences writing is preparation for this activity. However, the time when the student feels that he has enough data stored in a filing cabinet, in a computer, on charts, or in his head to justify tackling a chapter (or at least a major portion of one) is taken as the starting point. It is at this stage that there will be real appreciation of the existence of a systematically compiled set of records with cross classification where appropriate.

Preparation may be broken down into the four elements of Figure 8.2 from which it will be seen that it is proposed that the first step should be to plan the detailed order of the chapter sections.

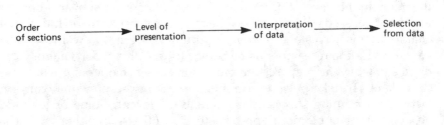

Figure 8.2   Preparing to write: the steps

1. Section Order and Demarcation The ordering of the sections of a chapter is a continuation of the process of logically structuring the report. Take as an example 'Survey of prior research' and consider the number of different ways in which the survey may be presented: chronologically, categorically, sequentially, in order of perceived importance; these are all possibilities. For example let the case of the student who is researching into factors affecting the success of computer marketing models be taken up again. He could divide his chapter on prior research in computer marketing research models into a whole range of sets of sections, a few of which are indicated in Figure 8.3 (restricted in each case to three sections for simplicity).

Although any of the Figure 8.3 orderings may be acceptable for short student reports they would constitute a poor approach to be adopted by a research degree student. A more appropriate basis might be:

1. The extent and range of computer applications in marketing;
2. Major successes and failures of computer based marketing applications
3. Suggestions in the literature for new computer based developments in marketing.

A decision on the nature of the major chapter sections will not be sufficient for the student to commence writing the body of the text. It will be necessary to continue the process of sub-division once or even twice further. The way in which this is done will have a considerable influence on the impact which the thesis will make. Again a number of options are available with, probably, categorical and chronological ordering being most appropriate in the marketing example being used. Thus major section 1 may be sub-divided into market planning, advertising, and logistics, each of which in turn may be discussed under the headings of early applications, applications during the 1960s and 1970s, and recent developments, as suggested by Figure 8.3.

Detailed guidance on format is often provided by the student's institution. Thus chapter titles may be required to be typed upper case and centred, main sections typed using initial capitals only, and commencing at the left hand margin, and so on. Probably the most appropriate (and least ambiguous) method of referring to each separate section is to use hierarchical numbering. This enables the student's approach to the logical breakdown of his writings to be clearly seen, particularly in the contents page. Thus if in our example 'Survey of prior research' is the second chapter of the thesis the early sections of that chapter would

BASIS OF SECTIONS

Chronological	Categorical		Sequential	Perceived importance
	(a)	(b)		
1. Early applications	1. Applications in N. America	1. Market planning models	1. Market research	1. Sales models
2. Applications during the 1960s and 1970s	2. Applications in other developed countries	2. Advertising models	2. Market planning	2. Advertising models
3. Recent developments	3. Applications in developing countries	3. Logistics models	3. Implementing market decisions	3. Planning models

Figure 8.3   An example of different section ordering within chapters

appear in the contents page numbered as:

2. Survey of prior research
2.1 The extent and range of computer applications in marketing
2.1.1. Market planning
2.1.1.1. Early applications

It is not customary to sub-divide chapters further than indicated in the example; to do this would result in too fragmented an approach causing the reader to be in some difficulty in remaining with the main theme being propounded. The writer nevertheless will still have much ordering to do and this, in large part, will be linked to the remaining three steps of Figure 8.2 (level of presentation, interpretation of data, and selection from data).

2. Level of Presentation The 'level of presentation' is not determined by the importance or status of the reader but by the location of the written account on a scale ranging from summary to comprehensive. As the point in writing student reports is to demonstrate knowledge and ability it is evident that they must aim for comprehensiveness. The criteria listed in Figure 8.1 imply that at the level of the research degree argument must be supported in every detail, leaving the student who must comply with a constraint on length in some difficulty as to what can be included. Below research degree level limitations on wordage will also often operate but in these cases the student can resort to the use of 'space precludes . . .' realising that he may be called upon to support any claims which he has made in writing at an oral examination. The research degree student (certainly the doctoral student) will have to undergo an oral examination. This, along North American lines, is often viewed as a 'thesis defence'. The student must always have this in mind during his writing and in his draft chapters should include all supportive evidence needed. The defence of his argument should however be concerned with the methodologies which he employed, the value claimed for his findings, and his recommendations for future work, and not with explaining and justifying the omission of corroborative material which should have been included in his thesis. If, therefore, it is felt that the thesis will probably be too lengthy it may be decided to omit whole sections (and justify the omission if called upon at an oral examination) rather than to reduce the level of detail throughout the text. If a student is unhappy at the thought of taking a prior decision to delete sections he may choose to write in an unconstrained manner in the knowledge that by editing substantial reductions in length may be possible.

Nevertheless the student should not pose himself an impossible task. Coverage in depth clearly reduces the scope for breadth of discussion and some students do encounter problems by attempting too broad a canvas. As well as leading to excessive length such an approach also carries the risk of superficiality. A page budget specifying the number of pages to be devoted to each section is a useful device for identifying this problem in advance. Amongst the possible cures are:

a) the researcher becomes less ambitious;
b) the researcher relies more heavily on summaries and reviews by previous authors rather than attempting to evaluate peripherally related areas of previous work;
c) reference is made to the student's own work published elsewhere;
d) whole sections may be omitted.

Obviously an indispensable aid in this is for the student to be clear about the relative importance he assigns to the different topics he would ideally wish to tackle.

3. Interpretation of Data Student report writing is a very specific form of communication, with the final product usually forming a one-to-one link between the student and his examiner. Particular note must therefore be taken of interpretation of data. The student should always be conscious of the person or type of person who will be responsible for evaluating his work. Obviously if the examiner is on the staff of the student's institution and there is no external assessment it behoves the student to seek guidance before he commences writing. If external assessment is involved it is part of British tradition that there shall be no contact between student and examiner, but this should not preclude the student from making 'behind the scenes' enquiries to establish whether the examiner has any pronounced views on writing or content. Research degree students who accept the advice that writing should commence as early in their research as possible may at that time not know who their external examiner will be. They will, therefore, have little on which to base their interpretation, other than that the person will probably be of some academic distinction and will be familiar with the technicalities and jargon of a particular field. Only if the student leaves the field should it be necessary therefore to supply definitions.

It may perhaps appear to be a little cynical to give much stress to the need to seek to satisfy the examiner of the report. Research theses in particular should after all be seen as an addition to the general body of knowledge; available to all. The student is nevertheless undertaking an examination and his primary objective to achieve success is quite clear; the publication of books and articles based on the material contained within the research report will come later.

4. Selection from the Data As a process this is part of the writing itself, but the student may need to take a prior decision on a number of issues. Chapter 6 indicated that by the time the student has completed his reading, data collection and analysis this will have resulted in the accumulation of a mass of data held in one form or another. The problem is to transform the data into a well ordered, appropriately interpreted account written at the requisite level.

Although the student should have been selective at the data gathering phase some material will probably be superfluous to the requirements of the report. For example if the fieldwork has involved a large sample survey it would be inappropriate to include all completed questionnaires in the report (although these should be retained as primary source material which may be called for at an oral examination); and one example of the questionnaire should of course be included. On the other hand if, say, several in-depth interviews have been tape-recorded it would be desirable to include the transcripts of each of these in an appendix. Again computer based statistical analyses will probably lead to many different outputs. If a representative example of a set of outputs conveys the point the researcher wishes to make then there is no need to include every page of output in the report.

In purely scientific terms an important question with doctoral theses is the degree to which the findings would be repeatable if the work were to be undertaken by another researcher. This implies that as well as an adequate description of the methods of analysis employed, (very possibly including computer program listings) primary data should ideally also be made available to the reader. At present the latter requirement tends to be honoured in the breach and readers are reminded of the observations made in Chapter 6 on how the researcher might make his data more widely available.

Taking into account comments made earlier on the level of presentation a reasonable rule for research degree students to follow is that if there is any doubt as to whether a particular piece of data should be included, then include it; deletion is always possible at the editing stage.

The writing itself

Student endeavour in all other directions will come to nought if he is unable to transcribe his research experience into a form which will meet the requirements of the qualification he is pursuing. As it could well be the first occasion on which he has tackled a job of such magnitude and as he will most probably lack the expertise of the professional report writer it follows that he should provide tangible evidence of his strengths and shortcomings to his supervisor and colleagues as early in the study as possible. Only by putting his thoughts in writing will he be able to generate the constructive criticism which will assist him in satisfying the criteria put forward earlier in this chapter. There still remains, however, the problems of what to say, in what order and how ideas should be expressed. The first two are to do with the organisation of sections and the last, although obviously involving style as discussed above, will be considered more broadly as the presentation of ideas.

1. Organisation of Sections It was suggested above that it is usually undesirable to divide a chapter into more than sub-sub-sections. The example used above led to 'Early applications' (of the computer in marketing) being a sub-sub-section, but having decided upon his chapter content the student should not be tempted to launch himself into writing without a good deal of further planning.

First he must ask himself what is the purpose of the particular section of his report. How important is the section and how much space should be devoted to it? How comparative, descriptive, critical should it be? Should comprehensive coverage be attempted or would it be sensible to start by deciding that only the US and the UK will be considered? Having selected market planning as a category how should this be defined? The implications of a chronological approach, with sub-section 2.1.1.2 covering the 1960s and 1970s means that 'early' refers to the pre-1960 period; is this sensible or should the first period extend to 1965 or even 1970? Is segmentation by industry desirable?

What might have seemed at first sight to be a simple and straightforward narrative task is now seen as being far from it. Any attempt by the student to write without decisions on structuring will almost inevitably lead to lengthy periods staring into space, followed by much crossing out, insertions and the gradual accumulation of screwed-up paper. To avoid this happening he should write down all the points (including *aide memoires)* which may be of relevance in no particular order, and from these select those which will be used and place them in order; for example:

Definition of market planning
Brief account of early computing technology as applied to business
Adopt a comparative approach as far as possible, USA *v* UK, industry by industry. Use as source material leading marketing, management science and planning journals of UK origin, supplemented by private communications.

Having decided upon the ground to be covered the student should then treat each portion of his report which has its own heading as a mini-chapter in which he should:

a) make an introductory statement;
b) provide background information;
c) supply data (often in the form of figures and tables);
d) undertake analysis;
e) summarise the analysis;
f) reach some conclusions.

Even if no further partitioning of the data by the use of 1, 2, 3 and so on or i), ii), iii), is attempted the reader will readily appreciate that the student has planned his writing if he organises his sections in this way.

2. Presentation of Ideas It is recommended that in order to improve the digestibility of his writings the student should try and develop a good style. It is, however, appreciated that this is not acquired easily. Nevertheless there are a number of basic factors of presentation with which the student should be familiar. Monroe, Meredith and Fisher (1977) refer to these as 'stimulus-response' patterns in their book *The Science of Scientific Writing* which, although addressed to scientists, makes many points of general relevance. Some common patterns which they select are:

Question-Answer When you generate a question in writing, the reader will expect you to answer the question – soon.
Problem-Solution If you present a problem the reader will expect a solution or an explanation of why no solution is forthcoming.
Cause-Effect, Effect-Cause Whether you have mentioned a cause first or an effect first, once you have mentioned one, the reader will surely expect you to mention the other.
General-Specific When you make a general statement, the reader will expect to be supplied with specifics, which clarify, qualify, or explain the general statement.

Although the presentation of ideas is the very nub of the process of writing there is little that can be added here except, again, to encourage students to devote some of their time to reading literature which has been written specifically on the topic of report writing. It should always be remembered that the research report is a communication and that the response of greatest interest to the student will be whether or not it has reached the required standard. At research degree level it will not be possible to assess beforehand the reaction of the examiner and it is therefore essential that a comparable level of criticism is obtained from another source. Obviously there will be much dependence on the supervisor but this should not preclude the student from seeking expert opinion elsewhere. Though the student will certainly wish to take the advice of other researchers familiar with his own field it should be remembered that the layman is often able to spot illogicalities or omissions in the argument and is likely to prove a good touchstone for the evaluation of style. Thus the acknowledgements to colleagues, spouses and friends that are customary in most research reports are usually far more than a courteous formality.

The student should not be too disappointed if his first attempts to convey his ideas and arguments are heavily criticised. An obvious conclusion is that time is needed to develop the requisite skills and reinforces the need to commence writing as early as is feasible. If the person were an experienced communicator on research then much redendancy would be avoided by leaving the writing until the analysis has been completed; but the student will rarely fall into this category.

Editing

Although notes of guidance for prospective contributors are provided by publishers most of the latter employ editors who modify scripts so that they conform with what is known as 'house style' but who also may often virtually rewrite the material submitted around the ideas it contains. Earlier students were advised to familiarise themselves with the style requirements of their institution but here a few suggestions are made about editing in the broader sense.

It is not uncommon to find supervisors who are prepared to act as editors, but this is not one of the responsibilities that the student can expect them to assume. Although the supervisor will normally approve a thesis or dissertation before it is sent to the external examiner this may be based on a broad view which is taken of structure and content. In this event, or when a supervisor has not been appointed, it behoves the student to determine his own strategy towards editing.

It is suggested above that in writing a research report for examination the student should tend to include rather than exclude material which may support his arguments. If this policy has been adopted it is reasonable to assume that when all the chapters have been written there will be much scope for pruning. It has been found that it is possible to make arguments with the same (even greater) force when papers have had to be reduced in length by as much as 50 per cent. Certainly there would be very few publishers willing to print doctoral theses in their entirety, being of the opinion, that proportionate savings in costs achieved by a reduction in length would much exceed the proportionate force of argument lost; certainly for the first ten or twenty per cent reduction in length.

Students have control over the length of their reports and if they feel, despite the attractions of conciseness, that there is little scope for reduction that is a decision they may take. Editing is, however, not simply a matter of eliminating text but is designed to ensure that the research findings are rewritten and presented in as effective a manner as is possible. Much of this chapter so far has been taken up in prescribing what the student should seek to achieve, but there remains the need to stand back from what has been written and assess it both in broad and specific terms. Although editing will probably be undertaken continuously the two levels of the individual chapter, and of the full report will be considered:

1. Editing the Individual Chapter The first draft of a chapter will be either handwritten or typed by the student. Typing competence is sometimes possessed by students but usually the final version of the report is completed by a skilled typist. On occasions the student may feel inclined to have draft chapters typed and particularly in these cases it is clear that substantial changes to the text should be avoided as far as possible. Before a chapter is passed for professional typing it should therefore be carefully edited.

Monroe, Meredith, and Fisher (1977) have suggested that good style emerges from naming, predicating and modifying. The first two of these are the basis of the 'core' elements of a sentence, which comprise the subject, verb and object. The core is then expanded by adding modifiers:

a) inflation is created (the core idea);
b) inflation is created by excessive wage demands (the core idea has been modified);
c) inflation is created by excessive wage demands rather than by an increase in money supply (the modifier has been modified).

With each sentence being made up of a core idea and modifiers Monroe, Meredith and Fisher then proceed to recommend a procedure for editing:

1. *Underline the core elements of every sentence.* Find the subject, the verb, and the object of the sentence. If there is more than one subject, verb, or object, underline all of them.
2. *Look for the core idea.* Make sure that the main idea is expressed in the core of the sentence and that this basic idea makes sense *by itself.*
3. *Check for modifiers between the core elements.* As a general rule, ten or more words between the subject and the verb is too many.
4. *Look for misplaced modifiers.* When you come across a potential problem, draw an arrow from the modifier to what it modifies. A long arrow means that you should rework the sentence.
5. *Check items for precision.* Have you defined the specialised terms? Examine all words representing qualitative judgements. Check to make sure that you've used these correctly, that the reader will understand what *specific* qualities are being summed up in each word.

The writers then examine the way in which sentences are assembled to form paragraphs and consider the changes that alterations in one sentence may necessitate in others. Monroe *et al* are primarily concerned with the writing of articles. Obviously the sentence-by-sentence procedure proposed above should not be applied to a lengthy report. Its value in the context of the latter is that the student could with advantage apply it to his early writing as one way of improving style.

In the above way readability should be enhanced but it must be borne in mind that this will not in itself guarantee quality of argument. The student should be prepared to undertake a substantial rewrite of sections of his chapter if the whole reads unsatisfactorily. In doctoral or part-time research an interval of perhaps two years may have elapsed between the writing of early chapters on the literature survey and research methodology and the final chapters on analysis and the conclusions. It is assumed that throughout these longer studies supplementary notes will have been appended to chapters as further insights are gained. Editing will include the task of incorporating additional and newer material into the body of the text.

Sometimes so much appears on a particular topic that the student finds it almost impossible to keep abreast of what is being published let alone incorporate it into his own thesis. Often such flurries of interest are ephemeral being perhaps occasioned by a centenary or something similar. Under those circumstances provided he does not fear being 'scooped' the researcher is probably best advised to sit it out and hope to complete his work once interest has died down. In other cases the only advice that can be given is that he calls a halt to further data gathering and analysis and then as rapidly as possible, that is within a few months, completes his report and submits it for examination, before his knowledge becomes out of date. The dangers of this type of project particularly for the part-time researcher were indicated in Chapter 2. It is considered that many good pieces of doctoral research are never completed for this reason. Furthermore all students at whatever level face the problem to some degree. The final version of the report cannot be written satisfactorily without a clear view of its structure both overall and chapter by chapter, and this cannot be attained if other research activities are still continuing.

2. **Editing the Full Report** If the procedure recommended, namely researching and writing simultaneously has been followed the student will eventually have assembled all the sections of his report from Chapter 1 to the list of references. It is to be hoped that students with supervisors will have obtained regular guidance and that this will be reflected in the writing. Neither the student nor the supervisor will, however, be able to assess the whole report until the last section has been written and it is important that plans for final editing are clear.

Depending upon the goodwill of the supervisor it may be that the latter will read the final report, make suggestions as to how it should be edited, and then repeat the process through a series of iterations until the product is deemed to be acceptable. If, of course, editing (that is, rewriting) is insufficient and additional analysis is called for, project completion may be delayed significantly. If the student cannot expect more than one careful reading from his supervisor it is logical that this should be done after the student has undertaken what he sees as necessary editing of the full report. In the absence of a supervisor the whole responsibility rests with the student although he may be able to prevail upon an acquaintance (including a staff member) to assist him.

The research degree student will appreciate that although his thesis will be examined as an exclusively individual effort (unless collaborative work is acknowledged) a bad fail will reflect adversely on his supervisor. This would be the case particularly if it is evident that little guidance has been given, as for example when original conclusions have been poorly presented.

In the later section on preparing for an oral examination a checklist for evaluating a research report is presented. Many of the questions raised are pertinent to the editing process.

Proofreading

This is the final stage of writing before the report is put into its covers. In publishing, a 'proof' is original text which has been typeset, and proofreading is the process in which typeset material is checked for deviation from the original copy. Two types of errors are recognised; 'author's' when the writer wishes to change his material and 'literals' which are mistakes which arise in typesetting. The usual practice is for the proofreader to use different inks to distinguish between the two types of error and various symbols are used to indicate the nature of an error.

The student will normally be communicating directly with a typist and will understand the need to ensure that his instructions are clearly understood. Although every time he rereads his report there is a considerable likelihood that he will wish to edit it further the concern here is with errors made by the typist. It can be profoundly irritating to a reader if he continues to encounter mistakes of this nature.

Every student who writes a report for presentation should, therefore, endeavour to ensure that at least in the typographical sense it is perfect. Unfortunately 100 per cent sampling of a large number of items (here, words) is not 100 per cent efficient. It is not, however, unrealistic to expect that no less than 98 per cent of pages should be error free and that if this figure drops to 95 per cent the student can expect adverse comment from the examiner.

Usually proofreading is undertaken by the student himself. The rules are fairly obvious:

a) read each line in turn;
b) recognise that intense concentration is needed and break off as soon as attention starts to wander;
c) read aloud;
d) take a sample (say 5 per cent) of those pages on which no errors have been noted and reread them.

Particular attention should be paid to spelling errors and faults in grammar; and to inconsistencies, for example, where the same reference is cited with a variety of different dates, and to omissions. As an encouragement at this tedious stage of the writing the student should recognise that in contrast to the irritation created by numerous typographical mistakes readers are much impressed by text which is virtually error free.

THE PREFACE

There may be a number of observations which the student would like to make which are not part of the research proper. Included are introductory or explanatory remarks which the student would communicate verbally if he had the opportunity. Most readers prefer sight of a report before discussing it with the writer and it is important to attempt to avoid misconceptions or to pre-empt criticism through the use of a preface, which, it is hoped, will be read before the body of the report itself.

Although the preface provides an opportunity for the student to make personal statements it is still necessary to know where the line should be drawn. Thus, although the external examiner may be told that the research was interrupted for three months due to a doctoral student breaking a leg playing rugby, this is not information which will be of relevance to the world at large. It would, however, be acceptable to imply that the time available for the research had been reduced by finding an initial topic unprofitable before turning to the research which is to be reported on. Similarly it would be in order for a doctoral student to refer to the fact that a foundation for the research had been achieved by the completion of a dissertation in a similar field for the purpose of satisfying the requirements of a master's level course involving taught courses and a short research project.

If joint work has been involved the extent of the collaboration can be clearly stated in the preface. This leads to acknowledgements which as a matter of courtesy should range from academic to material helpers. In the former category would come experts in the subject area who may have carried no responsibility for the student but gave of their time to advise him, or perhaps computer specialists who put considerable effort into sorting out some of the difficulties which are often encountered in using or developing software. Material help may include the typists who very often will have to struggle with raw and amended copy to an extent well beyond that which any payment might justify. The supervisor should of course justify acknowledgement on several counts if he has carried out his responsibilities effectively.

REPRODUCING THE REPORT

Proofreading is, of course, just one aspect of an important last stage of the report where the several copies required by the institution's regulations and the student himself are reproduced from the original copy. In all save the most unusual circumstances the bulk of the report will have been typed and will then be photocopied as necessary. Since it is one of these copies that will go to the examiner the impression created by it is important. In particular it makes little sense to devote enormous care to structuring, editing and proofreading the report and then to obscure this by presenting a finished article which has been poorly reproduced.

There are a number of factors that affect the appearance of the final copies. Firstly, only the most exceptional typist can produce an acceptable original on a manual typewriter. An electric machine offers a much more even quality of print. Secondly, portable machines tend to have poor registration and therefore corrections are more likely to show because the corrected text is slightly out of line with the original. Furthermore an office machine is more likely to provide the half-line registration that is essential in the typing of mathematical or statistical formulae. All in all then there is much to be said for having the report typed on an electric typewriter particularly of the 'golf ball' type which permits a variety of different typefaces (including mathematical symbols) to be used. In this way good quality original text can be secured.

As well as textual material, however, most research reports will contain a variety of tables, drawings and graphs. Where the tables are produced as a by-product of a computer analysis it obviously reduces the chances of error to get them produced directly by the computer. It is also likely to involve less work for the student and typist to do things this way. The student who has acquired computing skills is therefore probably well advised to design his computer output so that it can go directly into the thesis. Where possible the computer output should be printed on a letter quality printer. Usually, however, it will be printed on a line printer and a few points are worth bearing in mind. Other things being equal slow line printers (about 300 lines per minute) produce better quality output than fast ones (about 1,000 lines per minute). Secondly, a line printer ribbon only lasts a few hours and produces much better copy at the start of that period than at the end. Thirdly, line printer output copies better if printed onto a plain white background. Thus where the installation uses lined stationery it is better to get the paper reversed so that printing is on the plain back of the paper. In many installations it will probably be possible to ensure that the final copies of tables are printed as 'specials' taking these points into consideration since only the most exceptional thesis will require the printing of more than a few dozen tables and then only once. This of course assumes that the student has been prudent enough to save computer files of the relevant outputs so that all the tables can finally be printed at one time.

Slightly less familiar, but in the authors' experience of greater value in producing a high quality final text, are computer graphics; these take a variety of forms. Graphs and pictures may be obtained on microfilm or from photographs of visual display units. The most usual way of producing them however is on a computer graph plotter. The output of such plotters is comparable with that attained by a skilled draughtsman and requires only a few minutes of time on the graph plotter and a few seconds of computer time. They are well suited to the production of simple histograms and charts or to far more complex diagrams such as maps and are available on most larger educational computer systems. Most plotters work in several colours (though without access to a colour Xerox this facility is probably best used sparingly). There are a variety of computer packages available that make the use of such plotters relatively easy. Figure 8.4 shows, for instance, a computer plotted graph generated by the SIMPLEPLOT package (Butland, 1981) available at many educational institutions in the UK and abroad.

Not all diagrams lend themselves to being drawn using the computer. Traditionally in scientific work they are drawn using cartridge or similar pen and mapping ink. However, this is not something that the previously inexperienced student can hope to do successfully himself and therefore if the diagram needs to be drawn this way it will probably be necessary to approach a professional draughtsman. The problems in doing this are that as well as being a fairly costly process it can be a slow one. The alternative approach that can be carried out by the student himself is to make use of rub on transfers such as Letraset to produce special symbols, lines, and so on. If produced larger than required and then photoreduced a very professional diagram can be produced quite quickly.

Copying

Once the finished text is assembled it needs to be copied. Provided joins and edges are covered with liberal quantities of proprietary erasing fluids they will not show in the final copy so that the original can well be assembled by gluing several sheets together. What is usually more important is that the various parts of a composite original be similar in contrast and this may require ingenious preliminaries with the 'light original' button or contrast control on the copier to make sure the various sections are of similar density.

Not all photocopiers have such facilities, and it may well be worth seeking out a sophisticated copier to run off copies of those few pages that always cause inordinate trouble to reproduce. If, as will often be the case it offers photoreduction facilities so much the better, since certain diagrams and computer output need to be reduced in size to fit into the standard A4 format likely to be specified in most sets of UK regulations.

Sometimes a student will wish to include photographs in his report. One possibility is to paste prints into each of his copies; alternatively the

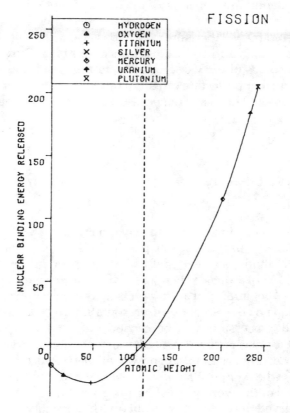

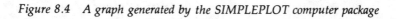

Figure 8.4   A graph generated by the SIMPLEPLOT computer package

photographs may be contained within a folder. To create the best effect the student may wish to reproduce the photographs. Photocopying will produce poor results and indeed printers have to resort to a special screening process for good results. In the latter case the prints are photographed through a glass screen ruled with a fine grid which separates the illustration into small dots to simulate the shades of grey. If the student decides to follow this course he will need to find someone (probably a graphic designer) with the necessary equipment.

Many students are subject to nightmare visions of draft chapters or even the whole draft report being destroyed in a fire or left on a train. Such accidents do happen and are perhaps more likely than might be expected in what is often a somewhat stressful period of research. The sensible student will therefore exploit the ease with which copies can now be produced to insure against disasters of this type. Provided there are at least two copies of the work in different physical locations, one should survive. Further protection can often be obtained by producing a copy for the supervisor. This helps to speed up the process of getting drafts read anyway.

WORD PROCESSING

Word processing provides a way of producing research reports of far higher quality than is usually possible. Good presentation has some impact on almost any external examiner; poor presentation, as noted earlier, certainly does. Therefore, the existence of word processing facilities is beginning, if nothing else, to increase external examiners' expectations of the standard of presentation to be achieved.

Word processing may be carried out on a computer specifically intended for that purpose. More importantly for most research students word processing programs are now available on microcomputers such as the PET or the APPLE. Essentially text is typed into the computer under the control of the word processing program. Once a satisfactory text has been achieved the text is printed out on a high quality printer again under control of the word processing package. Usually the text will be typed in over some considerable period and stored on magnetic tape or diskette so that it can be embellished or corrected as desired. A good word processing package provides a number of facilities, namely:

| Editing functions | Moving sections of text from one part to another |

	Replacing all occurrences of a word or phrase by another
	Insertion or deletion of text
Typographical functions	Automatic margin setting
	Space adjustment to align margins
	Automatic hyphenation
	Automatic pagination

Sophisticated packages offer a number of features such as the automatic numbering of sections and figures and the ability to renumber if sections are added or deleted, the compilation of an index and possibly the detection of spelling mistakes.

For the student author and his supervisor the editing functions have considerable potential. It has already been suggested in the section on style that at least in the early stages of writing up the student or his supervisor may well feel that much rearrangement is needed to enable the student to present his arguments as logically and as forcefully as possible. Thus it is not at all unusual to find that material that is incorporated in one of the later chapters (which may well have been written first) would in fact be better split and incorporated in one or more earlier chapters. In practice this becomes increasingly difficult to do as more and more of the text is typed and it is probably fair to say that the final form of many research reports is often affected more than the student would wish by the practical problems of getting material retyped. A word processing package allows not merely the movement of sections of text from one part of the report to another but also permits the insertion of the bridge passages that this frequently necessitates and the removal of redundant sentences. The ability to correct all occurrences of errors such as consistently spelling 'consistent' as 'consistant' is again extremely useful in improving the quality of the text. Such errors often unfairly create a very poor impression of the quality of the research. Luckily most students have specific spelling problems rather than general ones and probably need at most only to replace the incorrect version of a couple of dozen words. On a more positive note the same feature can usually be used to provide an index since the word processor can find all occurrences of a specified term in the text and print out the numbers of the relevant pages. Equally where inspiration strikes late in the day an inferior technical term can be replaced by a more appropriate one.

The typographical functions give the final version a very professional look. Margins, line spacings, and so on can be set to whatever standard is required by the institution. The automatic adjustment of spaces between words to align both left and right hand margins gives a most attractive 'book like' quality. As an additional bonus the author can run his report off in a different format to that specified for examination purposes, for example, single lined on A5 paper. It is likely that the use of word processing packages will become relatively commonplace over the next few years.

PREPARING FOR AN ORAL EXAMINATION

It is possible that at all levels of writing, whether report, dissertation, or thesis, the student will be called upon to meet one or more examiners in order to defend his conclusions verbally; the award of a PhD will certainly involve this. However long it may last, the oral examination will only require a fraction of the time that the research project as a whole will take. Nevertheless it is far from a formality and the wise student will accordingly prepare for it as thoroughly as he can with a view to confirming the high opinion that the examiners should already have conceived of his research from the study of his written report.

The sensible student will at the earliest possible stage have done homework on his examiners and will have attempted to accommodate in his writing the implications of any preferences and attitudes which they are thought to hold. It is not too cynical to suggest either, particularly at doctoral level when the examiner will be an expert in the field, that references to the examiner's own work should be made. The academic world is of course well known for its conflicts of opinion on topics and the doctoral student should do his best to ensure that there will be no antipathy towards him simply because of the line of argument he has pursued.

The student should hope therefore that although he will be confronted by examiners who will seek to ensure that academic standards are safeguarded his examination will be unbiased. And, that if his writing satisfies the relevant criteria listed in Figure 8.1 he will, given a convincing performance under oral examination, be successful. The listed criteria do not, however, provide sufficient information as to the details of what should have been achieved. The student should attempt to place himself in the position of the examiner and consider the type of question which he may put in order to evaluate the report. To provide the student with a systematic basis for anticipating how his research may be evaluated, a number of questions under each of the eight criteria of Figure 8.1 are posed which the doctoral student should seek to satisfy. To do this a checklist proposed by Hansen .and Waterman (1966) is drawn upon in part. In relating it to his own situation the student may find it useful to remember that for higher degrees individual examiners may well seek the advice of colleagues on particular aspects of the research outside their own sphere of interest.

1. *Evidence of an original investigation or the testing of ideas*
   a) Was the aim of the research clearly described?
   b) Were the hypotheses to be tested, questions to be answered, or methods to be developed clearly stated?
   c) Was the relationship between the current and previous research in related topic areas defined, with similarities and differences stressed?
   d) Are the nature and extent of the original contribution clear?

2. *Competence in independent work or experimentation*
   a) Was the methodology employed appropriate? Was its use justified and was the way it was applied adequately described?
   b) Were variables that might influence the study recognised and either controlled in the research design or properly measured?
   c) Were valid and reliable instruments used to collect the data?
   d) Was there evidence of care and accuracy in recording and summarising the data?
   e) Is evidence displayed of knowledge of and the ability to use all relevant data sources?
   f) Were limitations inherent in the study recognised and stated?
   g) Were the conclusions reached justifiable in the light of the data and the way they were analysed?

3. *An understanding of appropriate techniques*
   a) Given the facilities available, did it seem that the best possible techniques were employed to gather and analyse data?
   b) Was full justification given for the use of the techniques selected and were they adequately described? In particular were they properly related to the stated aims of the research?

4. *Ability to make critical use of published work and source materials*
   a) Was the literature referenced pertinent to the research?
   b) To what extent could general reference to the literature be criticised on the grounds of insufficiency or excessiveness?
   c) Was evidence presented of skills in searching the literature?

d) Was due credit given to previous workers for ideas and techniques used by the author?

e) Is evidence displayed of the ability to identify key items in the literature and to compare, contrast and critically review them?

5. *Appreciation of the relationship of the special theme to the wider field of knowledge*

a) Was the relationsip between the current and previous research in related topic areas defined, with similarities and differences stressed?

b) Was literature in related disciplines reviewed?

c) Was an attempt made to present previous work within an overall conceptual framework and in a systematic way?

6. *Worthy, in part, of publication*

a) Was the organisation of the report logical and was the style attractive?

b) With appropriate extraction and editing could the basis of articles or a book be identified?

7. *Originality as shown by the topic researched or the methodology employed*

a) To what extent was the topic selected novel?

b) Was there evidence of innovation in research methodology compared with previous practice in the field?

8. *Distinct contribution to knowledge*

a) What new material was reported?

b) To what extent would the new material be perceived as a valuable addition to a field of knowledge?

c) To what extent do the conclusions overturn or challenge previous beliefs?

e) Were the findings compared with the findings of any similar studies?

f) Was the new contribution clearly delimited and prospects for further work identified?

g) To what extent does the work open up whole new areas for future research?

The student should rehearse his answers to an appropriate selection from the above list of questions. This procedure should indicate what additional evidence will need to be taken into the examination. In the main any supplementary material will relate to the data gathering and analytical phases, but may also include papers which the student has written during his research.

Whatever the level of the examination it should go without saying that the student if called upon will be able to defend, explain, elaborate, or even apologise for any part of it. In the last mentioned respect tolerance which may be extended towards the undergraduate is unlikely to apply in the case of the doctoral student. If an unacceptable weakness is found by such a student after a thesis has been submitted criticism is best anticipated and coped with by preparing a typed statement for distribution at the start of the examination.

THE ORAL EXAMINATION

Though practice varies depending on the level of the research project the oral examination will almost always involve at least two and possibly several examiners. Usually there will be at least one external examiner present for a postgraduate project and this may also be the case at undergraduate level. In some universities the supervisor will during the oral examination function as an internal examiner which will imply a definite difference in his attitude to that to which the student has been accustomed. In other universities the role of internal examiner may be taken by one or more members of staff perhaps with the supervisor's formal role being that of 'in attendance'. In addition for a research project that has involved collaboration with outside bodies various people not on the staff of the institution may also function as examiners.

It should be appreciated by the research student that the prime purpose of an oral examination is to satisfy the examiners that the report presented represents individual or acceptably collaborative effort. If collaboration has been involved evidence of the degree of co-operation may be requested.

Whether or not the report is the student's own work is fairly quickly established and the main concern of the examiners is to ensure that any claims made in writing can be justified and that the analytical methods used are understood. In part the examiners are adding credibility to the report by approving it, particularly in the case of the research thesis which will then be included in bibliographies. During the examination, however, the student should expect to have to express opinion on topics which he may feel are peripheral to his studies in order to convince the examiners of his expertise in the wider field which includes his area of study. Although well able to defend his written arguments uncertainty as to where the discussion might lead may give cause for prior concern. In particular, the student's craftmanship and honesty are to some extent on trial as well as the merit of the research report.

As far as preparation is concerned the individual student must decide what best suits him. It is obviously sensible however to set aside as long a period of time beforehand if at all possible so that he can get himself into the right frame of mind for the oral examination and refamiliarise himself with the details of a research report that may have been completed several weeks before. To provide such a period is most likely to cause difficulty for the part-time student or the student who is now working in a full-time job both of whom are likely to have many other demands on their time. Perhaps the best mental preparation is to be in a position to exploit the strengths of his writing and to pre-empt criticism of its weaknesses. Obviously the advice of a friend or colleague or even better a rehearsal for the oral examination can be of great help here. The doctoral student should be able to remind himself that insofar as his conclusions are concerned they will be original. He should have developed considerable expertise in his chosen topic area and it should be possible for him to defend his thesis from a position of some strength. He must, however, expect questions which probe the scope of the topic, the nature of the target population, the type of cross-sectional comparison selected, and so on at whatever level is appropriate for the type of research he has been conducting.

With regard to the examination itself possibly the most important advice that can be offered is that the student should not attempt to 'pull the wool' over the examiners' eyes. Very rarely will it be possible to get away with this in front of experts. As suggested above it is far better that the student should admit to his shortcomings even if this means that in part the report will have to be rewritten.

Initially at least the meeting will be conducted by the examiners with the student playing a very reactive role. At this stage it is important that the student answer concisely but completely the questions put to him by the examiners, since the nature of his replies will be taken as a guide to the way in which the research itself was conducted. Therefore, where he is uncertain as to exactly what is meant by a question the student should request further clarification before attempting to answer. Nor where the question is difficult or subtle should he hesitate to reflect so that he can give a considered reply. It should also be remembered that the examiners are likely to concentrate on what they perceive to be the key strengths and weaknesses of the work and that the various examiners may differ as to what these are. Accordingly the student must anticipate that discussion will range widely and that questions will be posed on many different aspects of the research. If the student is confident about his work and findings and when he judges that he has achieved sufficient rapport with the examiners there could well be advantage in the student becoming more positive; warming as it were to his theme.

SUMMARY

> EVALUATION OF A RESEARCH REPORT: will involve certain criteria with which the student should be familiar according to the level of his research.

> THE WRITTEN ACCOUNT OF RESEARCH: should be of sufficient quality in respect of : structure
> : style
> : content.

> THE QUALITY OF REPRODUCTION: of a report can be an important factor in influencing an examiner and should be given full consideration.

> AN ORAL EXAMINATION: should be carefully planned for and the student should rehearse answers to questions which might be put to him.

Epilogue

And now with the chosen research topic successfully completed what benefits accrue? Since this has been written for students there should be a tangible reward in the form of a degree or diploma for which the research formed all or part of the requirements. This will undoubtedly have career benefits particularly at the higher levels of research where they will be construed by others as evidence of the student's ability to carry out a substantial study requiring inventiveness, expertise and perseverance.

It is to be regretted that despite the potential for achieving a reputation through the dissemination of a student's research findings these often remain imprisoned in a thesis or a dissertation stored on a library shelf. However, the successful student may well wish to make his work more widely available and indeed may be encouraged to seek publication by requests for copies from researchers working in the same field.

Research students in the USA have long had (since 1938) a further option available in the dissertations publishing service provided by University Microfilms International of Ann Arbor. This service has been available to UK authors for several years. A publication fee is charged which covers the cost of microfilming the thesis to produce a master microfilm copy held by UMI, from which microform or paper copies may then be produced on demand. This system is economical since no initial print-run has to be created as in conventional ink-on-paper publication. In addition, it means that the work need never go out of print and that it is perpetuated in the bibliographical support publications of that programme such as *Comprehensive Dissertations Index*. Researchers who may wish to publish only an abstract of their thesis can obtain details of submission procedures for UMI's European abstracts journal, *Dissertation Abstracts International, Section C*.

The successful research project can form the basis eventually of a substantial reputation earned through books and articles derived from it and research the student may carry out later. Sometimes it may be many years afterwards that a change of job or a slight alteration in career direction may provide an opportunity to utilise knowledge and skills gained during the research. Be that as it may the immediate and substantial benefit that accrues to any student comes from the learning that is provided to a greater or lesser extent by any research project. For however good his supervisor and no matter what help he got from others, the successful student will have displayed, and also enhanced his ability to carry out intellectually demanding work independently.

An Example of Topic Analysis

Topic Analysis

Student:

Area of proposed study: The contribution of UK graduate engineers to innovation since 1945

Date:

1 Hypothesis or research objective

Samuel Smiles in his *The Lives of the Engineers* (1878) wrote 'In a word Smeaton knew how to improve but Watt knew how to create'. Further, Smiles was much concerned with the need to turn ideas into commercial reality and so implied four major dimensions of the job of the engineer:

Invention
Improvement
Entrepreneurship
Management

These dimensions may also be taken as the main elements of innovation (Bright, 1964).

This study will not attempt to hypothesise that UK engineers have or have not made a specific contribution to innovation but will seek to identify and describe the role of graduate engineers in innovation (and any trends in it) from the end of the Second World War to the present. The study will be confined to areas of interest of corporate members of the Council of Engineering Institutions (CEI).

2. Prior research in the area

Much has been written about the training and careers of engineers in the UK and during the last two decades many studies and surveys have been conducted in this area. These range from a survey of Mechanical Engineers conducted by Hutton and Gerstl (1964) in 1962 to the biennial Surveys of Professional Engineers by the CEI, the latest of which appeared during 1981. Contributors to the field included the British Association for the Advancement of Science (1977), the Engineering Employers Association (1977), Berthoud and Smith (1980), and the Finniston Committee (1980). From these it is possible to gain a reasonable insight into the role of the engineer in both society and industry and to comprehend the environmental constraints and opportunities which have a bearing on this role. But none of these surveys gives much insight into the job of the graduate engineer and his involvement in innovation.

Similarly a great deal of effort has been put into the measurement of innovation (for example, OECD, 1971) and into identifying its sources (for example, Jewkes *et al.*, 1969). Two major approaches have been used:

i) analyses of changes in the rate of innovation (usually based on patent statistics);
ii) case studies of individual innovations.

Authors such as Mensch (1976) split innovation into Basic and Secondary forms which assists in classification but still leaves the researcher in the field with an enormous amount of ground to cover. Freeman (1973) reporting on the work of the Science Policy Research Unit at the University of Sussex referred to various roles in the process of innovation, namely: 'technical innovator', 'business innovator', 'chief executive', and 'product champion'. There is an obvious connection between these roles and the four major dimensions of innovation listed above which may be of value in data collection. This project will attempt to examine the process of innovation by studying a professional group whose job is generally perceived to be concerned with innovation. The literature of professions, (cf. Whittington, 1979) is therefore also expected to be relevant.

3. Value in research terms of the possible outcomes

As stated the research will be 'descriptive' in nature and will stand or fall on the extent to which it can add convincingly to knowledge about how engineers contribute to innovation. The research would appear to be fairly symmetrical since quite contradictory views exist of the quantitative and qualitative contributions which engineers have, during recent decades, made to UK economic life; thus:

> there is a growing proportion of those (engineers) with only poor or mediocre talent. This is illustrated in terms of such factors as poor personal motivation and little professional commitment; a lack of flexibility, breadth of vision and creativity in problem solving; need of close supervision; and deficiencies in inter-personal and communicative skills (The Select Committee on Science and Technology, 1976).

and:

> Government must convince society that the engineer and industrialist can and do contribute to the welfare, well being and growth of the nation (British Association for the Advancement of Science, 1977).

Furthermore novelty is claimed in attempting to link the graduate engineer with innovation.

If as expected the research tends to support one or other of the opinions quoted above it should still have value as a basis for further comparative studies. Thus is may be possible for other researchers to extend the study to examine the engineer and his contribution to innovation in other industralised economies. It could also be used in a study within the UK designed to establish who are responsible for innovations; graduate engineers, qualified scientists and engineers (a broader body including graduate engineers), or other groups.

4. Probable methodology or approach to the research

Data on which the research findings will be based will be obtained from a survey of graduates in English, Welsh, and Scottish universities who have retained membership of one of the engineering institutions. To assist in the identification of trends and to establish the effect of career experience on innovation only universities in existence in 1950 will be included in the sample. This will enable cohorts of engineers who graduated in 1955, 1965, and 1975 to be approached.

The data gathering instrument will be a mailed questionnaire which, in large part, will comprise limited choice questions directed at obtaining information such as job history, involvement in new business ventures, the securing of patents, the licensing of technology, and the development of new products and processes.

The problem of response is recognised and to this end it is intended to focus where possible on graduates of schools of chemical, civil, electrical, and mechanical engineering. Collaboration will be sought from the CEI and the relevant corporate institutions. A total sample size of 1,200 is envisaged, which will enable questionnaires to be sent to 100 of each of the four types of engineer in the three cohorts.

The major objectives of the analysis would be to:

a) measure the contribution of the graduate engineer to innovation;
b) describe the jobs of various types of graduate engineer and the way they develop during their careers;

and on the basis of these findings, assess likely future changes in the contribution of engineers to innovation and in the requirements for engineering training.

It is expected that the analysis will rely heavily on statistical methods aimed at detecting the effect of length of work experience and type of engineering qualification on a number of variables of interest, such as number of patents held by the respondent. It is also hoped to elucidate differences between the jobs and experience of the different types of graduate engineers by means of cluster analysis and scaling techniques. Finally, it is proposed that an attempt be made to identify a number of 'typical' career patterns for graduate engineers.

5. References

Although omitted here references should in practice be included in a topic analysis.

A Select Bibliography on Analysis

CONTENT ANALYSIS

Holsti O.R., *Content Analysis for the Social Sciences and Humanities,* 1969.
   Comprehensive account of purposes of and techniques for analysing the content of text material. Clear discussions of a variety of applications with particular reference to the overall place of content analysis and the problems encountered. Good discussion of the principles of use of the computer in content analysis.

GENERAL STATISTICAL TEXTS (O LEVEL (16+)STANDARD MATHEMATICS)

Spiegel M., *Theory and Problems of Statistics*, 1972.
A standard introductory text based on worked examples. Covers regression but not experimental design.

Yeomans K.A., *Applied Statistics: Statistics for the Social Scientist*, 1968.
Similar coverage to Spiegel, but with a certain amount on econometrics and operational research. Standard textbook approach with much fuller discussion of the uses of particular techniques. Useful to any researcher, not merely social scientists.

Christensen H.B., *Statistics Step by Step*, 1977
Systematic approach, carefully organised and extending as far as experimental design.

Green P.E. and Tull D.S., *Research for Marketing Decisions*, 1978.
Requires knowledge of elementary statistics but otherwise little mathematical expertise. Remarkably comprehensive coverage of the underlying concepts and marketing applications of many different multivariate techniques including regression, experimental design, discriminant analysis, cluster analysis, etc. Particularly good on multidimensional and other scaling techniques. Very useful to researchers in any field who are willing to make the effort to translate the examples into a context relevant to their research.

GENERAL STATISTICAL TEXTS (A LEVEL (18+) STANDARD MATHEMATICS)

Klecka, W.R., Nie N.H. and Hull C.H., *SPSS Primer*, 1975
Guide to the most widely available computer statistical analysis package together with a brief account of theory and applications of each technique. Even non social scientists may well find the package the easiest way of carrying out statistical analyses. Many of its programs were written for the analysis of biomedical data.

Open University Course MDT241 Team, *Statistics an Interdisciplinary Approach*, 1974.

In conjunction with the associated set books an excellent introductory course including regression but not experimental design. Good on applications. Suitable for persevering O level student.

Sage Publications series, *Quantitative Applications in the Social Sciences*

Series of books covering individual techniques of interest to social scientists, e.g. factor analysis, path analysis.

Phillips L.D., *Bayesian Statistics for Social Scientists*, 1973.

Bayesian methods and ideas are becoming increasingly important in research. They were not, however, for reasons of brevity discussed explicitly in Chapter 5. This reference provides a clear account of the basic ideas. Of interest to researchers outside the social sciences also.

GENERAL STATISTICAL TEXTS (FIRST YEAR UNIVERSITY MATHEMATICS)

Box G.E.O. and Tiao G.C., *Bayesian Inference in Statistical Analysis*, 1973

Gives a complete Bayesian theory of statistical inference.

Johnson N. and Leone F., *Statistics and Experimental Design in Engineering and the Physical Sciences*, 1964.

The title gives a good idea of the contents. Text also includes useful brief account of discriminant analysis.

Kendall M.G. and Stewart A., *The Advanced Theory of Statistics*, 1966.

Very comprehensive treatment of most branches of statistics though newer ideas such as multidimensional scaling are not covered. A standard text.

C.A. O'Muircheartaigh and Payne C. (eds) *The Analysis of Survey Data*, 1977.

Covers most multivariate statistical techniques with the exception of experimental design, plus certain related topics. Each chapter written by individual experts. Good on pitfalls of techniques as well as applications.

Unless otherwise stated the following references to specific methods require A level standard mathematics.

FACTOR ANALYSIS

Harman H.H., *Modern Factor Analysis*, 1967.
  Guide to statistics of factor analysis.
Rummell R. J., *Applied Factor Analysis*, 1970.
  Similar to above but more orientated towards applications.

DISCRIMINANT ANALYSIS

Goldstein M. and Dillon W.R., *Discrete Disciminant Analysis*, Wiley, 1978.
  Presents wider range of classification methods in less depth.

Lachenbruch P.A., *Discriminant Analysis*, 1975
  Covers practical application of classical techniques of discriminant analysis.

CLUSTER ANALYSIS

Anderberg M.R., *Cluster Analysis for Applications*, 1973.
  Self-explanatory title. Gives computer programs.

Everitt B., *Graphical Techniques for Multivariate Data*, 1978.
  Describes a number of different techniques of clustering with a strong emphasis on visual presentation. Also of interest from point of view of pattern recognition.

SCALING

Maranell G.M. (ed.), *Scaling: A Sourcebook for behavioural scientists*, 1974
  Set of readings on older approaches to scaling including theory and methods of construction and including useful discussions of idea of measurement.

Shepard R.N., Romney A.K., Nerlov S.B., *Multidimensional scaling*, 1972.

More recent work in scaling has been to develop scales to measure objects along two or more dimensions. This is a two volume work containing papers delivered at a seminar. Volume 1 contains papers which provide a comprehensive coverage of the theory of the subject plus a substantial bibliography. Volume II describes applications in a number of different fields of research ranging from linguistics to marketing.

van der Ven A.H.G.S., *Introduction to Scaling*, 1980.
Clear account of both the underlying ideas and the applications of various unidimensional and multidimensional scaling techniques.

PATTERN RECOGNITION

Batchelor B.G. (ed.), *Pattern Recognition*, 1978.
Set of conference papers on a variety of different computer methods for pattern recognition. A number of papers require first year university or even higher standard mathematics.

Everitt B., *Graphical Techniques for Multivariate Data*, 1978.

Granger, C.W.J., and Hatanaka, M., *Spectral Analysis of Time Series*, 1964.
Correlation functions are of considerable importance in pattern recognition particularly in recognising patterns over time. This book illustrates their use in a context that should be understandable to most researchers. First year university mathematics required.

EXPERIMENTAL DESIGN MODEL

Campbell D.T. and Stanley J.C., *Experimental and Quasi Experimental Designs for Research*, 1966
Clear non-statistical discussion of ideas underlying experimental design model and of ways of extending it to field studies where not all factor levels can be controlled.

Cox D.R., *Planning of Experiments*, 1958.
Clear description of statistics of experimental design methods with

wider range of applictions than Duckworth including a number of biomedical examples.

Duckworth W.E., *Statistical Techniques in Technological Research*, 1968.

Good on applications of and rationale underlying use of experimental design in field of technology.

Keppel G., *Design and Analysis: a researcher's handbook*, 1973.

A guide to the use of experimental design methods in practice with particular reference to applications in psychology.

PATH ANALYSIS

Blalock H.M. (ed.), *Models in the Social Sciences*, 1971.

Comprehensive set of readings on the topic. Though ideas are most likely to be of interest to non-experimental scientists they provide an adequate idea of the technique for any researcher.

REGRESSION ANALYSIS

Draper N.R. and Smith H., *Applied Regression Analysis*, 1980.

Standard reference work on the theory and application of regression methods. Needs first year university mathematics.

Freund R.J. and Minton P.D., *Regression Methods*, 1979.

Guide to use of regression methods with particular reference to facilities typically provided by computer programs. Needs first year university mathematics.

Klein L.R., *A textbook of econometrics*, 1974.

Econometricians are amongst the largest users of regression methods. Furthermore the applications of the technique are often sophisticated. This is one standard text that presents a picture of them. Needs first year university mathematics.

THEORY OF KNOWLEDGE

Cohen M.R. and Nagel E., *An Introduction to Logic and Scientific Method,* 1934.

A standard text on scientific method. Considers both experimental and observational studies and history. Useful discussion on principles of measurement.

Gardiner P.L., *Theories of History,* 1959.

Comprehensive set of readings on what is meant by historical knowledge with applications to other fields also.

Popper K., *The Logic of Scientific Discovery,* 1959.

The classic logical positivist account of scientific method including the doctrine of falsifiability..

GENERAL TEXTS ON RESEARCH METHODOLOGY

Fox D.J., *The Research Process in Education,* 1969.

Comprehensive coverage of variety of research methods for use in social sciences and humanities ranging from content analysis to the experimental design model. Particularly good on practical aspects of carrying out research of this type.

Kerlinger F.N., *Behavourial Research : a conceptual approach,* 1979.

General discussion of the underlying philosophy of behavioural and related research plus useful introduction to discriminant analysis, factor analysis, experimental design, etc.

Struening E.L. and Guttentag M. (eds). *Handbook of Evaluation Research,* 1975.

Guide to research in the evaluation of social policy taking in many types of analysis and data collection methods particularly the experimental design model.

TEXTS ON SPECIFIC ASPECTS OF RESEARCH METHODOLOGY

Cook T.D. and Campbell D.T., *Quasi Experimentation*, 1979.
An examination of methodological problems of causal explanation based on field observations and ways of overcoming them.

Dubin R., *Theory Building*, 1969.
An examination of the construction of various types of theory in the social sciences but relevant to many other fields.

Glaser B.G. and Strauss A.L., *The Discovery of Grounded Theory*, 1967.
A key reference for the student engaged in exploratory research. Distinguished by its insistence on the interaction between datagathering and theory development. Also contains novel ideas on data sources. Intended for social scientists but of interest to all researchers making use of field observations.

Warwick D.P. and Osherson S. (eds) *Comparative Research Methods*. 1973.
Excellent set of readings on methodological problems in important area of social science research.

General Bibliography

Ackoff R.L., *The art of problem solving accompanied by Ackoff's fables*, Wiley, New York, 1978.

Anderberg M.R., *Cluster Analysis for Applications*, Academic Press New York, 1973.

Arts and Humanities Citation Index, Institute for Scientific Information Philadelphia, published three times a year.

ASLIB, *Index to Theses accepted for higher degrees by the Universities of Great Britain and Ireland and the Council for National Academic Awards*, ASLIB, London, published annually.

Batchelor B.G., *Pattern Recognition*, Plenum Press, New York, 1978.

Berdie D.R. and Anderson J.F., *Questionnaires: Design and Use*, Scarecrow Press, Metuchen, N.J., 1974.

Blalock H.M. (ed.)*Casual Models in the Social Sciences*, Macmillan, London, 1971.

BLLD *announcement bulletin*, British Library Lending Division, Boston Spa, Yorks, monthly.

Bolton N., *Concept Formation*, Pergamon, Oxford, 1977.

Box G.E.P. and Jenkins G.M., *Time Series Analysis : Forecasting and Control*, Holden-Day, San Francisco, 1976 (rev. edn)

Box G.E.P. and Tiao G.C., *Bayesian inference in statistical analysis*, Addison-Wesley, Reading, Mass., 1973.

British Museum, *General Catalogue of printed books*, British Museum, London.

British Standards Institute, *Recommendations for Citing Publications by Bibliographic References*, London, 1978.

Broehl, W.G. and Shurter R.L., *Business, research and report writing*, McGraw Hill, New York, 1965.

Butland J., *Simpleplot User's Handbook,* Report No. 253, University of Bradford School of Electrical and Electronic Engineering, 1981.

Campbell D.T. and Stanley J.T., *Experimental and Quasi-Experimental Designs for Research*, Rand McNally, Chicago, 1966.

Catalogue of British Offical Publications not Published by HMSO, Chadwyck Healey, Cambridge, UK.

Central Statistical Office, *Facts in Focus*, 4th edn, Penguin, Harmondsworth, 1978.

Christensen H.B., *Statistics Step by Step*, Houghton Mifflin, Boston, 1977.

Churchman C.W., Ackoff R., and Arnoff E.L., *Introduction to Operations Research*, Wiley, New York, 1957.

Cohen J., *Statistical Power Analysis for the Behavioural Sciences*, Academic Press, New York, 1969.

Cohen M.R. and Nagel E., *An introduction to logic and scientific method*, Routledge and Kegan Paul, London, 1934.

Committee of Public Accounts *Minutes of Evidence*, HMSO, London, May 1980.

Cook T.D. and Campbell D.T., *Quasi Experimentation : design and analyses issues for field settings*, Rand McNally, Chicago, 1979.

Cooper B.M., *Writing Technical Reports*, Penguin, Harmondsworth, 1964.

Cox D.R., *Planning of Experiments*, Wiley, New York, 1959.

De Bono E., *Teaching thinking*, Temple Smith, London, 1976.

Directory of British Associations CBD Research Ltd. Beckenham, Kent, published annually.

Dissertation Abstracts International, Ann Arbor, published monthly.

Dixon D., and Hills P., *Talking about your research,* Primary Communications Research Centre, University of Leicester, 1981.

Draper N.R. and Smith H., *Applied Regression Analysis*, 2nd edn, Wiley, New York, 1980.

Dubin R., *Theory Building*, Free Press, New York, 1969.

Duckworth W.E., *Statistical Techniques in Technological Research*, Methuen, London, 1968.

Ehrenberg A.S.C., *Data Reduction : analysing and interpreting statistical data,* Wiley-Interscience, London, 1975.

Encyclopedia Britannica, 15th edn, Encyclopedia Britannica, London, 1974.

Everitt B., *Graphical Techniques for Multivariate Data,* Heinemann, London, 1978.

Fox D.J., *The Research Process in Education,* Holt, Rinehart, Winston, New York, 1969.

Freund R.J. and Minton P.D., *Regression Methods,* Dekker, New York, 1979.

Gardiner P.L., *Theories of History,* Free Press, New York, 1959.

Glaser B.G. and Strauss A.L., *The discovery of grounded theory : strategies for qualitative research,* Weidenfeld and Nicholson, London, 1967.

Goldstein M. and Dillon W.R., *Discrete Discriminant Analysis,* Wiley, New York, 1978.

Gorden R.L., *Interviewing strategy, techniques and tactics,* Dorsey Press, Homewood, 111., 1969.

Gowers Sir E., *The Complete Plain Words,* HMSO, London, 1954.

GRAI — Government Reports, Announcements and Index, National Technical Information Service, Springfield, Va., published semi-monthly.

Granger C.W.J., and Hatanaka M., *Spectral Analysis of Time Series,* Princeton University Press, 1964.

Green P.E. and Tull D.S., *Research for Marketing Decisions,* 4th edn, Prentice Hall, Englewood Cliffs, 1978.

Gunning R., *The Technique of Clear Writing,* McGraw-Hill, New York, 1952

Hansen K.J. and Waterman R.C., *Evaluation of Research in Business Education,* National Business Education Quarterly, vol. 35, pp. 81–84, 1966.

Harman H.H., *Modern Factor Analysis,* rev. edn, University of Chicago, 1967.

Harvey J.M., *Statistics America: Sources for Market Research,* CBD Research Ltd, Beckenham, Kent, 1973.

Harvey J.M., *Statistics Europe : Sources for Social, Economic and Market Research,* Edition 3, CBD Research Ltd, Beckenham, Kent, 1976.

Holsti O.R., *Content Analysis for the Social Sciences and Humanities,* Addison-Wesley, Reading, Mass., 1969.

Howard K. (ed.), *Managing a Thesis,* University of Bradford Management Centre, 1978.

Jantsch E., *Technological Forecasting in Perspective,* OECD, Paris, 1967

Johnson N. and Leone F., *Statistics and Experimental Design in Engineering and the Physical Sciences,* vols. I and II, Wiley, New York, 1964.

Kendall M.G. and Stewart A., *The Advanced Theory of Statistics,* vols. I, II and III, Griffin, London, 1966.

Keppel G., *Design and Analysis : a researcher's handbook,* Prentice Hall,

Englewood Cliffs, 1973.

Kerlinger F.N., *Behavioural Research : a conceptual approach*, Holt, Rinehart and Wilson, New York, 1979.

Klecka W.R., Nie N.H., and Hull C.H., *SPSS Primer : Statistical Package for the Social Sciences Primer*, McGraw Hill, New York, 1975.

Klein, L.R., *A textbook of econometrics*, 2nd edn, Prentice Hall, Englewood Cliffs, 1974.

Lachenbruch P.A., *Discriminant Analysis*, Collier Macmillan, London, 1975.

Leedy P.D., *Reading Improvement for Adults*, McGraw Hill, New York, 1956.

Lockyer K.G., *An Introduction to Critical Path Analysis*, 3rd edn, Pitman, London, 1969.

Maranell G.M. (ed.), *Scaling : A Sourcebook for the Behavioural Scientist*, Aldine, Chicago, 1974

Mitchell B.R., *European historical statistics, 1750–1970*, Macmillan, London, 1975.

Mitchell B.R. and Deane P., *Abstract of British Historical Statistics*, Cambridge University Press, 1962.

Mitchell B.R. and Jones H.G., *Second Abstract of British Historical Statistics*, Cambridge University Press, 1971.

Monroe J. Meredith C. and Fisher K., *The Science of Scientific Writing*, Kendall/Hurst, Dubuque, Iowa, 1977.

Morgernstern O., *On the accuracy of economic observations*, 2nd edn, Princeton University Press, 1963.

Moser C.A. and Kalton G., *Survey methods in social investigation*, 2nd edn, Heinemann, London, 1971.

Naroll R., *Data Quality Control : A new research technique*, Free Press, New York, 1962.

O'Muircheartaigh C.A. and Payne C., (eds) *The Analysis of Survey Data*, vols. I, II, Wiley, New York, 1977.

Open University Course MDT241 Team, *Statistics an Interdisciplinary approach*, Units 1-11, 13-16, 1975, Open University, 1974.

Open University Course D291, *Statistical Sources*, Units 1-16, Open University, 1975.

Pemberton J.E., *British Official Publications*, 2nd edn, Pergamon, Oxford, 1973.

Phillips L.D., *Bayesian Statistics for Social Scientists*, Nelson, London, 1973.

Pickett K.G., *Sources of Official Data*, Longman, London, 1974.

Popper K.R., *The Logic of Scientific Method*, Hutchinson, London, 1959.

Research In British Universities, Polytechnics and Colleges, 3 vols. 2nd edn, British Library, London, 1981.

Research Index, Business Surveys Ltd. Dorking, Surrey, published fortnightly.

Rummel J.F. and Ballaine W.C., *Research Methodology in Business,* Harper and Row, New York, 1963.

Rummel R.J., *Applied Factor Analysis,* North Western Press, Evanston, 1970.

Sage University Papers, *Series: Quantitative Applications in the Social Sciences,* Sage Publications, Beverley Hills.

Sawin D.B., Langlois J.H. and Leitner E.F., *What do you do after you say hello? Observing, coding and analyzing parent-infant interactions,* Behaviour Research Methods and Instrumentation, vol. 9, 5, pp. 425-428, 1977.

Science Citation Index, Institute for Scientific Information, Philadelphia, published three times a year.

Shephard R.N., Romney A.K., and Nerlove S.B., *Multidimensional Scaling, theory and applications in the behavourial sciences,* vols. I and II, Seminar Press, New York, 1972.

Simon J.L., *Basic Research Methods in Social Science,* vols I and II, Random House, New York, 1969.

Social Science Citation Index, Institute for Scientific Information, Philadelphia, published three times a year.

Som R.K., *A manual of sampling techniques,* Heinemann, 1973.

Spiegel M., *Theory and Problems of Statistics,* SI edn, McGraw Hill, New York, 1972.

Spon's Architects' and Builders price book, Spon, London, published annually

STAR – Scientific Technical and Aerospace Reports, NASA, Washington, published semi-monthly

Stibic V., *Personal Documentation for professionals: Means and Methods,* North Holland, Amsterdam, 1980.

Struening E.L. and Guttentag M., (Eds.) *Handbook of Evaluation Research,* vols. 1 and 2, Sage Publications, Beverley Hills, 1975

Tarr G., *The management of problem-solving : positive results from productive thinking,* Macmillan, London, 1973

Times (The) *More than 200 student research awards to be stopped or cut after PhD completion rate study,* Times Newspapers, London, 15th January, 1981.

Times Index (The), Times Newspapers, London, published annually

Tomberg A., *EUSIDIC-Databases in Europe : a directory to machine readable databases and databanks in Europe,* ASLIB, London, 1978.

Turner R., (Ed.) *The Grants Register 1979-81,* Macmillan, London, 1978

United Nations Statistical Year Book, United Nations, New York, published annually

United States Library of Congress, *The National Union Catalog*

University of Bradford, *Calendar 1981-82*, University of Bradford, 1980

University of East Anglia, *1981-82 Calendar*, University of East Anglia, Norwich, 1981

University of Edinburgh, *Calendar 1981/82*, University of Edinburgh, 1981

van der Ven A.H.G.S., *Introduction to Scaling*, Wiley, New York, 1980

Walford A.J., *Guide to Reference Material*, Three Vols. Third Edition, Library Association, London, 1975

Warwick D.P. and Osherson S. (Eds.) *Comparative Research Methods*, Prentice Hall, Englewood Cliffs, 1973

Webb E.J., Campbell D.T., Schwartz R.D., and Sechrest L., *Unobtrusive Measures : Nonreactive research in the social sciences*, Rand·McNally, Chicago, 1966

Yeates D. (Ed.), *Basic training in systems analysis*. Pitman, London, 1971

Yeomans K.A., *Applied Statistics : Statistics for the Social Scientist, Vols. I and II*, Penguin Books, Harmondsworth, 1968

Index

236